DOS 5

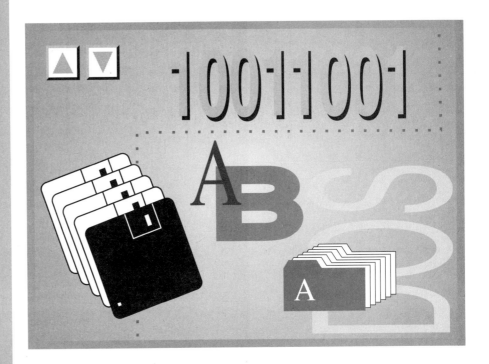

DOS 5

S.A.V.E. Edition

Dennis P. Curtin

REGENTS/PRENTICE HALL
Englewood Cliffs, New Jersey 07632

Library of Congress Cataloging-in-Publication Data

Curtin, Dennis P.
    [Microcomputers and DOS]
    DOS 5 / Dennis P. Curtin. — S.A.V.E. ed.
        p.   cm.
    Abridged ed. of: Microcomputers and DOS, 1993.
    Includes index.
    ISBN 0-13-045592-X (pbk.)
    1. MS-DOS (Computer file) 2. PC-DOS (Computer
file) I. Title.
QA76.5.C796 1993b
004.16—dc20   92-31089
                                                CIP

Acquisitions editor: Liz Kendall
Editorial/production supervision: Cecil Yarbrough
Copy editor: Robert Fiske
Designer and half-title illustrator: Janis Owens
Cover designer: Marianne Frasco
Interior art production: Dennis P. Curtin
Desktop publishing: Cathleen Morin
Prepress buyer: Ilene Levy
Manufacturing buyer: Ed O'Dougherty
Supplements editor: Cindy Harford
Editorial assistant: Jane Avery

© 1993 by REGENTS/PRENTICE HALL
A Division of Simon & Schuster
Englewood Cliffs, New Jersey 07632

Printed in the United States of America
10 9 8 7 6 5 4 3 2 1

ISBN 0-13-045592-X

Prentice-Hall International (UK) Limited, *London*
Prentice-Hall of Australia Pty. Limited, *Sydney*
Prentice-Hall of Canada Inc., *Toronto*
Prentice-Hall Hispanoamericana, S.A., *Mexico*
Prentice-Hall of India Private Limited, *New Delhi*
Prentice-Hall of Japan, Inc., *Tokyo*
Simon & Schuster Asia Ptd. Ltd., *Singapore*
Editora Prentice-Hall do Brasil, Ltda., *Rio de Janeiro*

CONTENTS

CONTENTS

P R E F A C E

Do You Need Incentive?
Workers who use computers, but who are similar in every other respect to workers who do not use them, earn a fat bonus of 10 to 15 percent for their knack with these machines.
The New York Times, *February 14, 1992, page D2, referring to a study by Alan B. Krueger of Princeton University.*

ASK THE AUTHOR

Dennis Curtin welcomes your questions about his textbooks and hardware and software issues. Please feel free to call him at 1-800-926-7074. For examination copies or ordering issues, call your Regents/ Prentice Hall representative.

Q U I E T !!
R E F E R E N C E
S E C T I O N

This text introduces you to the disk operating system known as DOS. DOS has been revised over the years. This book concentrates on DOS 5, the version introduced in 1992, but it takes note of earlier versions wherever they are different. As you proceed through the text, you will learn all of the basic concepts and procedures you need to understand in order to operate a computer. To simplify your introduction as much as possible, the text is organized into topics and chapters.

Topics: The Basic Unit

The basic unit of this text is the topic, a short section that is narrowly focused on a specific part of the computer or a specific DOS procedure. This narrow focus, and the precise beginning and end of a topic, make it easier for you to study than does a traditional chapter organization. Short topics are less intimidating than long chapters, and they make it easier for your instructor to assign specific sections.

Each of the topics contains the following elements:

- *Objectives* tell you what you should be able to accomplish when you have finished the topic.
- *Introductory concepts* introduce the basic principles discussed in the topic. These concepts all apply to DOS, but many also apply to other programs you will eventually use on a microcomputer. When you understand concepts, procedures are easier to learn because they fit into a framework. Understanding concepts also makes it much easier to transfer your understanding to other programs and other computers.
- *Tutorials* demonstrate step by step how to use the procedures discussed in the topic. If you follow the instructions, you quickly see how each procedure is performed and the results it has. This establishes a framework on which you can hang a better understanding of the procedures that are discussed in detail in the section that follows.
- The *Quick Reference* describes step by step how you execute commands. This section serves a dual function: You can refer to it when working on the activities in this text or when working on your own projects. Many of the procedures are presented step by step in highlighted KEY/Strokes boxes.
- *Exercises* provide you with additional opportunities to practice and gain experience with the concepts and procedures discussed in the topic. Unlike tutorials, the exercises do not guide you step by step. You have to determine the correct procedures to use.

Chapters: A Pause for Reinforcement

Related topics are grouped into chapters so you can pause to review and test yourself. At the end of each chapter are the following sections you should complete:

- A review of the key concepts and procedures that were discussed in the chapter.
- A series of questions that test your understanding of the concepts and procedures discussed in the chapter. There are three types of questions: fill in the blank, match the columns, and write out the answer.
- Projects that build skills and introduce problem solving. Background material is provided for each project, but no specific procedures are given. To complete the projects, you must already have mastered the topics in the chapter or go back and look up the information that you need.

Hands-On Lab Activities

In a lab-oriented course, your progress and enjoyment are highly dependent on the quality of the hands-on activities used as vehicles to teach you concepts and procedures. Ideally, these hands-on activities perform a number of useful functions.

- They build skills in the specific procedures you need to know.
- They demonstrate a variety of situations in which specific procedures are useful.
- They develop problem-solving skills. Exercises provide less guidance for you than tutorials, and projects provide even less. Moving though this sequence of activities challenges you to think about what you should do and why you need to do it.

This text includes dozens of such activities and presents them on three levels: tutorials, exercises, and projects. Each level requires an increasingly better understanding of DOS to complete it successfully.

- Tutorials introduce a specific procedure or a group of closely related procedures. Their purpose is to demonstrate how the procedures work and show the effects they have.
- Exercises at the end of each topic reinforce the concepts and procedures discussed in the topic. They focus on the topic of which they are a part. You will have to rely on your experience with the tutorial and refer to the Quick Reference section to find the information you need to complete exercises. This refines your ability to look up information you need to complete tasks—something you will have to do on your own when the class is over.
- Projects at the end of each chapter are like exercises, but require an understanding of more than one topic to complete them.

Key Features

This text has a number of features that distinguish it from other texts in this area.

- *A Jump-Start tutorial* lets you begin working on the computer from the very first day that you begin your study of DOS. This tutorial is designed to give you an idea of how the program works and demonstrate some of the things it can do.
- You will find that you first use this text to structure your learning and then later as a reference. To improve the text's usefulness as a reference, most procedures are presented step by step in highlighted KEY/Strokes boxes. By referring to the list of topics on the back cover, you can immediately locate a topic of interest and

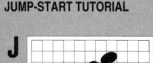

JUMP-START TUTORIAL

As the author of many books on computer applications, I teach teachers in seminars and workshops all over the country. If the room has computers, teachers are already punching keys while I'm still giving the introduction. Just like students, they can't wait to do something. The computer is an enticing, interactive tool, not a passive device you just read about. To encourage this hands-on flavor, the first topic in this text begins with a Jump-Start tutorial that lets you work with the computer and DOS as soon as possible. This tutorial not only lets you begin sooner but also shows you what the operating system can do.

PROBLEM SOLVING

It would be wonderful if the real world were structured like a textbook—with all of the necessary information neatly provided. Unfortunately, a boss rarely tells us to "copy all of today's files onto backup floppy disks to protect them and follow the instructions in the tutorial to do so." More often we are just told to back up our work as efficiently and quickly as possible. It's up to us to choose the tools and approach. This is problem solving, and it takes practice. The ideal classroom or lab activity will accomplish its primary goal of teaching procedures while at the same time introducing problem solving.

Student Resource Disks
Many of the files on which you work are on the *Student Resource Disk* which your instructor will make available to you.

then skim the Quick Reference section in that topic for the information that you need.

Getting Ready

Before proceeding with the activities in this text, consider these points:

■ You work only with files on a floppy disk. If your system has a hard disk drive, you use the DOS files stored on it, but you do not work with any of your own files on the hard drive. Making mistakes while doing so could cause problems on your system.

■ Occasionally, you will find references to "floppy disk systems" and "hard disk systems" in this text. By "floppy disk systems" we mean systems on which you run DOS from one floppy disk drive and save your work on a second. By "hard disk systems" we mean any system with DOS on the hard disk drive and at least one floppy disk drive.

■ DOS is published by Microsoft, and, as noted, it has been revised a number of times over the years. Moreover, a number of slightly different versions have also been produced for computer companies such as IBM and Compaq. Depending on which of these numerous revisions and different versions you are using, you may find that the prompts appearing on your screen vary slightly from those discussed in this text. If that happens, just be sure to read the screen carefully and proceed as instructed. In most, if not all cases, these variations will be minor and easily manageable.

The S.A.V.E. Series

This text is a Software Application Value Edition. It is part of the S.A.V.E. Series—a series of high-quality, value-priced books designed for use in computer courses with minimal lab time. Instructors can mix and match any combination of S.A.V.E. books to meet their course needs. These books can be used as lab supplements for Introduction to Computers texts or as main texts for short computer applications classes.

S.A.V.E. books are adapted from my COMPASS (Computer Application Software Series) Series texts. Each S.A.V.E. text has a COMPASS Series counterpart which includes advanced topics, a pocket guide, and a spiral binding. The COMPASS Series edition of this book is *Microcomputers and DOS: A Short Course*, second edition. It includes five topics on microcomputers and devices such as keyboards, display monitors, and printers, much of it in full color. *Microcomputers and DOS* also contains coverage of advanced DOS topics such as creating and using batch files, redirection and filters, and displaying and printing ASCII text files. COMPASS Series editions of application software texts include a real-world applications chapter and software keyboard templates. Contact your local Regents/Prentice Hall representative for a current list of the titles available in both the COMPASS and the S.A.V.E. series.

Supplements

The same complete supplements package available with the COMPASS texts is available to S.A.V.E. text adopters:

■ *Instructor's Manual with Tests and Resource Disks* by Donna M. Matherly contains suggested course outlines for a variety of

course lengths and formats, chapter summaries, teaching tips for each topic, competencies to be attained, solutions and answers to in-text activities, competency production tests, a test bank of objective questions, and a number of supplementary problems.

Two types of disks are included with this supplement, and both are available as either 3.5" or 5.25" disks.

- *Student Resource Disk* contains the unformatted files to be used to complete the hands-on activities in this text. This master disk can be duplicated for students. Arrangements can be made to have the *Student Resource Disk* bound to copies of this text for an additional fee—contact your REGENTS/PRENTICE-HALL representative to make arrangements.
- *Instructor's Resource Disk* contains files for chapter summaries, competencies, topic goals and tips, solutions for hands-on activities, competency tests, and supplementary problems.
- *Course Outlines on Disk* contains files and other information from the Instructor's Manual which allow the professor to customize lecture outlines and course syllabi with ease.
- Transparencies illustrate essential screen displays for DOS and Windows.
- *Test Manager* (3.5" and 5.25" disks) is a test-generating package that allows professors to customize the test questions contained in the Instructor's Manual. Users can edit, add to, and scramble test questions.
- A video covering DOS (Video Professor) is available to qualified adopters.

Acknowledgments

No book is the result of the efforts of a single person, and that is especially true of this text, where many people, from classroom instructors to printers, went the extra mile to create the best possible text. Although I accept full responsibility for any of the text's shortcomings, full credit for the things that were done correctly belongs to others.

The following teachers took time out of their busy schedules and traveled to another state to sit down with me in an all-day session. At that meeting they laid out a plan for me to follow to create the best possible revision of this text:

- Richard Bernardin, Cape Cod Community College
- Catherine Brotherton, Riverside Community College
- Linda Dowell, St. Johns River Community College
- Nancy P. Houston, Grove City College
- Sarah J. MacArthur
- James A. Pope, Old Dominion University
- Howard Pullman, Youngstown State University
- Frederick L. Wells, DeKalb College at Gwinnett Center
- Toni M. Hutto, Wake Technical Community College

A number of people reviewed the outline and/or the final manuscript with care and attention that the author had not previously seen. Many of these instructors spent days reading the manuscript and sharing their insights with the author. Their efforts often required that I reorganize and rewrite major sections of the text; and the final text has been greatly improved as a result.

- Nancy M. Acree, University of Puget Sound
- Richard Bernardin, Cape Cod Community College
- Catherine Brotherton, Riverside Community College
- Bruce Case, Thomas Jefferson High School
- Lee D. Cornell, Mankato State University
- Linda Dowell, St. Johns River Community College
- Deborah Haseltine, State Technical Institute at Memphis
- Dennis R. Heckman, Portland Community College
- Toni M. Hutto, Wake Technical Community College
- Donal Janes, Los Medanos College
- Donna M. Matherly, Tallahassee Community College
- Elise S. Patterson-Crate, Florida Community College
- James A. Pope, Old Dominion University
- Bonnie M. Skelton, Radford University
- Donna Yoder, Pima Community College

I would also like to express my appreciation to many others who helped me implement the plan for this text. The supplements that accompany this text were prepared by Donna Matherly. Her work expands on, and improves upon, the content of this text and she is a joy to work with. Robert Fiske and Donna Matherly tested all of the tutorials, exercises, and projects. They tried to chase down every error in concept or keystroke, and any that remain are not a result of their efforts.

Thanks also to all of those at REGENTS/PRENTICE HALL who brought the final result into print. Cecil Yarbrough coordinated all aspects of the book's production and worked as hard as anyone has ever worked to make it the best possible text. His efforts are greatly appreciated and are vividly illustrated in all aspects of this text. Liz Kendall helped plan the revision, coordinated all aspects of the project's development, and encouraged me over long months of writing and rewriting. Liz's assistant, Jane Avery, successfully juggled all of the reviewing and author contacts to keep information flowing well at all times. Without fail, when something was needed it was there. Cathy Morin electronically published the manuscript and worked side by side with me, laying out the pages and suggesting many improvements along the way.

Finally, this book is dedicated to Matthew Dennis Morin, who entertained (or distracted) me as much as possible during its development. His older sister, Emily, took over entertaining and distracting me when Matt was too tired to continue.

Dennis P. Curtin
Marblehead, Massachusetts

NOTATION USED IN QUICK REFERENCE COMMANDS

In this text, you will occasionally find notations such as **COPY A:**<*filename.ext*>**B:** or **REN** <*oldname.ext*> <*newname.ext*>. The names in brackets indicate the data that you should enter in your own commands. Substitute your own filenames for the brackets and the text within them. For example, if you see **COPY A:**<*filename.ext*>**B:**, enter **COPY A:MYFILE.WP5 B:**. If you see **REN** <*oldname.ext*> <*newname.ext*>, enter **REN JUMPSTRT.WP5 MYFILE.WP5**.

This text uses the following conventions for commands and prompts:

Commands

All keys you press (except those in boxes such as [Enter↵]) and all characters you type are shown in the typeface used here for **FILENAME**.

- Keys you press in sequence are separated by commas. For example, if you are to press [Y], release it, and press [Enter↵], the instructions read [Y], [Enter↵].
- Keys you press simultaneously are separeted by dashes. For example, if you are to hold down [Ctrl] while you press [PrtScr], the instructions read [Ctrl]-[PrtScr].

Prompts

All prompts, messages, and menu choices are shown *in this typeface*. When a prompt appears, read it carefully and do as it says.

Summary

Now that you have read about how keys and commands are presented, see if you can understand the following instructions:

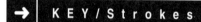

→ **KEY/Strokes**

To List the Files on a Disk

1. Insert the disk with the files to be listed into the drive.
2. Type *DIR* <drive:> and press [Enter↵].

To follow these instructions, you begin by inserting the disk with the files to be listed into one of the disk drives. If you insert the disk into drive A, you then type the command **DIR A:** and press [Enter↵]. If you insert the disk into drive B, you would type **DIR B:** and press [Enter↵].

DOS 5

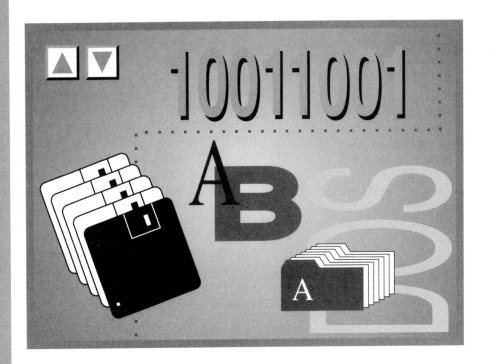

Getting Started with DOS

DOS—An Overview

After completing this topic, you will be able to:
- Load DOS on a floppy or hard disk system
- Determine the version number of DOS that your system is running
- Quit DOS and turn off your equipment

To use a computer, you must first load the operating system. This is called booting the system. The term *booting* comes from the expression "pulling oneself up by one's bootstraps." Once the operating system is loaded, you can load your application programs or use the operating system's commands to manage your files and disks.

If your computer is off, you load the operating system by turning it on. When you do so, the computer automatically looks to the startup drive for the operating system files that it needs to start up.

- On a floppy disk system, the startup drive is drive A, so you have to insert a disk that contains the operating system files into that drive.
- On a hard disk system, the startup drive is drive C, but the computer still looks to drive A first. Therefore, before you turn on a hard disk system, be sure to open the door to drive A or eject the disk so that the program does not try to load the operating system from that drive (see the section "Things That Can Go Wrong").

If the files it needs to start are on the disk in the startup drive, that disk is called a *system disk*. If the files are not on the disk in the startup drive, an error message is displayed, and the system will not boot.

Turning a computer on to boot it is called a cold boot. However, you can also reboot a computer if it is already on—called warm booting. To warm-boot the system, you hold down Ctrl and Alt and then press Del. (This command is usually written out as **Ctrl-Alt-Del**.). Warm booting clears all data from the computer's memory and has almost the same effect as turning the computer off and then back on again. You normally use this procedure only when you encounter a problem with your system. Whenever possible, you should exit any application program you are using before warm booting your system, or you may lose data.

In this tutorial, you take a quick guided tour of some of the most commonly used DOS procedures. You load DOS, check which version you are using, format a disk so that you can store your own work on it, explore directories, and copy files. Everything you do here will be explained in much greater detail later in this text, so relax. The purpose of this Jump-Start Tutorial is to get you over the initial hurdle of using DOS and to make it possible for you to perform basic procedures should the need arise at home, at work, or in other courses.

To load DOS on some systems, such as those connected to networks or with special startup menus, you follow procedures specific to your system. In these cases, ask your instructor how to display the DOS command prompt, and then start this tutorial at the section headed "Changing the Command Prompt."

GETTING STARTED

1. If your computer is on, turn it off. The location of the On/Off switch varies, but it may be located on the right side of the computer toward the rear.

2. Before proceeding:
   - If you are working on a hard disk system, open the door to drive A or eject the disk in that drive. Drive A is the name of the floppy drive if there is only one. If there are two (or more) drives, drive A is usually the one on the top or on the left.
   - If you are working on a floppy disk system, insert the DOS disk into drive A. If there are two (or more) drives, drive A is usually the one on the top or on the left. (On some systems, there may be more than one DOS disk. If you are working on such a system, the disk you use to boot the computer might be named the DOS startup, boot, or system disk. If you are unsure of which disk to use, ask.)

LOADING THE OPERATING SYSTEM

3. Turn on the computer. In a few moments, the computer may beep, and then drive A spins, and its light comes on while the operating system is loaded. If there is no disk in drive A, the computer looks to drive C for the program if the system contains a hard disk drive.
   - If a list of files is displayed, and the screen has the title *MS-DOS Shell*, *IBM DOS Shell*, or *Start Programs*, press F3 to display the command prompt.
   - If nothing appears on your screen, your display screen may not be on. On some systems, the display screen has a separate On/Off switch.
   - If your computer does not have a clock that is set automatically, in a moment the prompt reads *Enter new date:*. If this prompt appears, refer to the section "Entering or Changing the Date and Time" in the Quick Reference section of this topic.

   The command prompt appears and should read *C:\>, C>, C:\DOS>, A:\>, A>*, or something similar. This prompt indicates that DOS has been loaded.

LOOKING AHEAD: ENTERING COMMANDS

■ In all the instructions in this text, the characters you type are shown in upper-case letters, but whether you use uppercase or lowercase letters usually does not matter. For example, you can type **PROMPT PG** or **prompt pg**.

■ If you make a typo when entering any commands, press ←Bksp to delete the incorrect characters, and then type them in correctly before pressing Enter←┘.

LOOKING AHEAD: DEFAULT DRIVES

Most computers have more than one disk drive. For this reason, disks are assigned names: A, B, C, and so on. Just as you can be in only one place at a time, so it is for your computer. It is always on one and only one of the drives. The drive it is on is called the *default drive*. To have a command affect a disk in any other drive, you must indicate the letter of that drive in the command. This is called *addressing* the drive.

CHANGING THE COMMAND PROMPT

4. If your command prompt does not read *C:\>*, *C:\DOS>*, or *A:\>*, type **PROMPT PG** and press Enter←┘ so that it does (although the *DOS* part may be different).

CHECKING THE VERSION NUMBER

5. Type **VER** and press Enter←┘ to display the version number of the operating system you are using. Write it down so that you don't forget it. The commands you use vary somewhat depending on which version of DOS your system is running.

FORMATTING A DATA DISK

6. Locate a blank disk that **DOES NOT** contain any valuable files. The command you are about to use effectively erases all data from the disk.

7. Insert your disks as follows:
   ■ On a hard disk system, insert the blank disk into drive A.
   ■ On a floppy disk system with two disk drives, insert the DOS disk into drive A and the blank disk into drive B.

8. Set your drives as follows:
   ■ On a hard disk system, type **C:** and press Enter←┘ to change the default drive to drive C. The command prompt should read *C:\>* or *C:\DOS>*.
   ■ On a floppy disk system, type **A:** and press Enter←┘ to change the default drive to drive A. The command prompt should read *A:\>*.

9. Enter the FORMAT command as follows:
   ■ On a hard disk system, type **FORMAT A:** and press Enter←┘.
   ■ On a floppy disk system, type **FORMAT B:** and press Enter←┘.

   In a moment, a prompt asks you to insert a disk into the drive you entered in the FORMAT command and press or strike Enter←┘ when ready. You already inserted the disks in a previous step. (If you get the message *Bad command or filename*, or something similar, ask your instructor on what disk or in which directory the FORMAT.COM file can be found, and insert that disk or ask how you change to that directory.)

10. Press Enter←┘, and the drive spins as it formats the disk. (On DOS 4 and later versions, a message on the screen keeps you posted on the progress.) When the message reads *Format complete*, the drive stops.

11. If you are using DOS 4 or a later version, you are prompted to enter a volume label. Type your last name (abbreviate to 11 characters if necessary), and press Enter←┘ to continue.)

12. When the prompt reads *Format another (Y/N)?*, press N and then press Enter←┘.

EXPLORING YOUR STUDENT RESOURCE DISK

13. Insert the *Student Resource Disk* into drive A. (The *Student Resource Disk* is a special disk that contains all the files you need to complete the tutorials and exercises in this text.)

Disks can store a lot of files. To keep them organized, experienced users divide the disk into directories that are like file folders in which related files can be stored. Knowing which directory a file is in is important since you may not be able to run a program or copy a file unless you do. Directories are discussed in detail in Topic 9. For now, think of them as an address. Just as you may live in San Francisco in the state of California, a file may be stored in a directory named DOS on a drive named C.

WRITE PROTECTION

A disk must not be write-protected when you copy files to it.
■ To remove write protection from a 5¼-inch floppy disk, remove the tape covering the write-protect notch.
■ To remove write protection from a 3½-inch floppy disk, close the sliding tab in the write-protect window.

14. Type **A:** and press ⏎ to change the default drive to A, and the command prompt reads *A:\>*.

15. Type **DIR** and press ⏎ to list the directories on the disk. Directories are like file folders in which you can store related files. They are used to organize your work and programs on the disk. You can tell 1-2-3, DBASE, DOS, EXCHANGE, and WP51 are directories because they are followed by the notation *<DIR>*.

16. Type **CD \DOS** and press ⏎ The prompt changes to *A:\DOS>* to indicate that DOS on drive A is the current directory.

17. Type **DIR** and press ⏎ to display a list of the files in the DOS directory along with information about each file. The list is too long to be displayed on the screen, so the topmost files scroll off the top. However, notice how each file has a name such as WHATSUP, an extension such as DOC, a size (in bytes), a date, and a time.

18. Type **DIR/W** and press ⏎ to display the filenames in five columns without additional information so that more names can be displayed at one time.

19. Type **CD \DBASE** and press ⏎ to move to the DBASE directory.

20. Type **DIR** and press ⏎ to display a list of the files in that directory.

21. Type **CD \DOS** and press ⏎ to return to the DOS directory.

22. Type **DIR *.DOC** and press ⏎. The command told DOS to list any file with a period followed by the three letters DOC.

COPYING FILES

23. Type **COPY *.* A:** and press ⏎ to copy all the files from the DOS directory to A:\, the topmost directory on the disk—called the *root directory*. Files are listed on the screen as they are copied, and when all have been copied, the command prompt reappears. The *.* (called star-dot-star) part of the command uses wildcards to tell DOS "all files."

24. Type **DIR** and press ⏎ to see that all the files are still in the DOS directory.

25. Type **CD ** and press ⏎ to move back up to the root directory. The command prompt should change to A:\> to indicate that you are there.

26. Type **DIR** and press ⏎ to see that copies of all the files that were in the DOS directory are now in the root directory.

FINISHING UP

27. Either continue to the next activity or quit for the day. To quit, remove your disks from the drives and turn off the computer.

QUICK REFERENCE

You have to load the operating system only once during a session. If you are already running an application program, you use the application program's Quit or Exit command to return to the operating system or the menu from which you loaded the program.

→ KEY/Strokes

Loading DOS

1. Set your disk drives as follows:
   - To boot from a hard disk, open the door to drive A or eject any disk from the drive.
   - To boot from a floppy disk, insert a system disk (a disk with the DOS files needed to start up the computer) into drive A.
2. Turn on the computer. What happens next depends on how your system has been set up. Any of the following events may happen:
   - If your system's clock is not set automatically, you are prompted to enter the date and time each time you turn it on. If you are prompted to do so, see the section "Entering or Changing the Date and Time."
   - If your system is connected to a network, or has been customized, a menu may appear on the screen listing actions you can take.
   - The command prompt may appear and will normally be A> or A:\> if you booted from a floppy disk or C:\> if you booted from a hard disk drive. However, the command prompt can be customized, so it may be different on your system. The command prompt tells you that DOS has been loaded, that the default, or active, disk drive is drive A or C; and that the drive is ready to receive commands. From this command prompt, you can execute all DOS commands or start application programs such as WordPerfect, Lotus 1-2-3, or dBASE.
   - The DOS Shell, a menu-operated screen, may appear on systems using DOS 4 or later versions. To display the command prompt from this Shell, press F3.

The DOS 5 Shell

DOS 4 and later versions contain a Shell with pull-down menus you can use to execute commands. This illustration shows the screen that appears when the DOS 5 Shell is loaded.

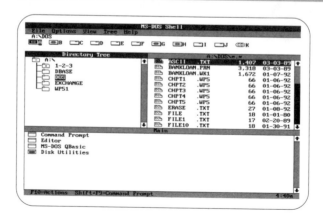

6   Chapter 1 · Getting Started with DOS

```
╔═══════════════════════════════╗
║      MAIN MENU                ║
║                               ║
║   1.  WordPerfect             ║
║   2.  Lotus 1-2-3             ║
║   3.  dBASE III Plus          ║
║   4.  DOS Command Prompt      ║
║   5.  E-Mail                  ║
║                               ║
║      Enter Choice: __         ║
╚═══════════════════════════════╝
```

Network Menus

Many computers are connected to networks so that they can communicate with one another. On these systems, special screens may appear that list programs you can run or commands you can execute.

MILITARY TIME

Versions of DOS prior to 4.0 do not recognize **a** and **p** after the time to indicate a.m. or p.m. With those versions, to set the computer's clock accurately in the afternoon or evening, so that its date will change at midnight, you must use military time. Military time is based on the 24-hour clock. In military time, the hours from 1 a.m. until noon have the same names as they do with the 12-hour clock. But at 1 p.m., the hour is 13:00 (called "thirteen hundred hours"); 2 p.m. is fourteen hundred hours; and so on until midnight, which is zero hours, when the sequence begins again.

Entering or Changing the Date and Time

When you first turn on some computers, you are prompted to enter the date and time. Entering the correct date and time is important because the computer's clock date-and-time-marks files that you save. The clock is also used by some programs to enter dates and times into files and to display them on the screen.

If you are prompted to enter the date, type it in the format MM-DD-YY, where MM (month) is a number from 1 to 12, DD (day) is a number from 1 to 31, and YY (year) is a number from 80 to 99 or from 1980 to 1999. For example, to enter the date January 10, 1993, type 1-10-93 and press [Enter←].

To enter the time when prompted to do so, use the format HH:MM, where HH (hours) is a number between 0 and 23, and MM (minutes) is a number between 0 and 59. For example, to set the clock to 1:30 p.m., type **13:30** (for military time—see box) and press [Enter←]. If you are using DOS 4 or later, you could also enter the time as 1:30p (for p.m.).

Things That Can Go Wrong

It is not at all likely that anything you type on a computer will really harm the system, but it is easy to make mistakes that affect your own work. That's why you should always keep backup copies of important files and take care to follow the directions in this text as you enter commands that are new to you. Here are some problems to look out for when working with DOS:

- When you boot an IBM computer system, you may see the error message *Non-System disk or disk error* (or a similar message on compatible computers). This appears when you turn on the computer with a disk in drive A that does not contain the operating system files that the computer needs. If you get this message, insert the DOS disk into drive A or open the drive's door if it is a hard disk system, and press [Enter←].
- The message *Bad command or filename* appears when you type a command incorrectly or when DOS cannot find the file you have tried to run. If you get this prompt, retype the command, or find a disk with the DOS utility program that you want to use.
- If you make a typo and notice it before you press [Enter←], press [←Bksp] to delete it, and then retype it.
- If you or the computer addresses a drive (for example, type **A:** and press [Enter←]) and the drive doesn't contain a disk, a message tells you the computer is not ready reading the drive and then offers you options to *abort*, *retry*, *fail*, or *ignore* (although the choices vary depending on the version of DOS you are using).
  - *Abort* cancels the command and returns you to the command prompt (or Shell).
  - *Retry* retries the command, perhaps after you have closed a drive door or inserted a disk.
  - *Fail* cancels the current portion of the command and then continues.
  - *Ignore* ignores the problem and continues processing the command.
- To cancel a command in progress, press [Ctrl]-[C] or [Ctrl]-[Break].

Quitting DOS

When you are done for the day, you should always exit the program you are using to return to the operating system, and then:

■ Open the floppy disk drive doors or eject the disks in the drives so that the disk drives' read/write heads don't leave indentations in the disks' surfaces.
■ Remove your disks from the disk drives to prevent their loss, increase security, and ensure that no one mistakenly erases them.
■ Turn off the computer or use the display monitor's controls to dim the screen so that an image will not be "burned" into its phosphor surface.

On some systems, after turning your computer off, you should wait 20 to 30 seconds before turning it back on. Some systems will not reboot without this pause. If you turn one of these systems back on too quickly, nothing happens.

►EXERCISES

EXERCISE 1

LOADING DOS ON YOUR OWN SYSTEM

Many computers are now networked or have other special startup procedures. If your system is one of these, list the steps here that you use to access the DOS command prompt so that you have it for future reference.

1. _____
   _____
2. _____
   _____
3. _____
   _____
4. _____
   _____
5. _____
   _____

EXERCISE 2

IDENTIFYING YOUR SYSTEM'S FLOPPY DISK DRIVES

If your system has more than one floppy disk drive, make a sketch of them and label them A, B, and so on. Use this sketch for later reference when you are asked to insert a disk into a specific floppy disk drive.

Executing Commands

After completing this topic, you will be able to:
- Describe the difference between internal and external commands
- Execute commands from the command prompt
- Print the screen display

Relax!
There is almost nothing that you can do from the keyboard that will damage the system or cause serious problems. If there were, it would be the system designer's fault and not yours.

DOS has a number of commands that you use to manage your files. You use these utilities to prepare disks for use on the computer and to copy, rename, erase, and otherwise manage files you have saved on your disks. These commands fall into two categories: internal commands and external commands.

Internal commands are available whenever the command prompt is displayed. Internal commands are automatically loaded into the computer's memory whenever you load DOS because they are included in the COMMAND.COM file that is loaded automatically whenever you boot the system.

External commands are stored on the DOS disk or hard disk until you need them. These commands are used less often than internal commands. Not loading them into memory until they are needed leaves room for other programs and data.

External commands are little more than small programs that are loaded into the computer's memory and then executed when you type their name and press Enter←. If you enter an external command and its program is not on the disk in the drive, the computer displays an error message indicating you have used a bad command. When this occurs, you first make sure you entered the correct command. If you did, you then use the DIR command (which you'll learn more about later) to check if the command's file is on the disk and, if not, locate the disk it is on. If you use an external command frequently, copying the appropriate program file from the DOS disk onto an application program disk may be helpful.

EXTERNAL COMMANDS ON HARD DISK SYSTEMS

This tutorial and all other DOS activities in this text assume that your hard disk system's AUTOEXEC.BAT file contains a PATH command listing the directory in which the DOS program files are stored. All hard disk external commands are given in this text without specifying the location of the DOS files needed to execute them.

Usually DOS files are stored in a directory of their own on the hard disk. As you may recall, directories are like file folders in which you can store related files. If you are working on a hard disk system, ask your instructor where the DOS files are stored and write down the name of the directory because you may need to know it to complete the activities in this text. Now, let's look at two ways you can execute DOS's external commands.

1. The best way to execute commands is to have the DOS directory listed in the PATH command in the AUTOEXEC.BAT file that the system reads when you boot it. Type **C:** and press Enter◄┘ to make drive C the default drive. Then, type **C:** and press Enter◄┘ to be sure you are in the topmost directory of drive C. Finally, type **TYPE AUTOEXEC.BAT** and press Enter◄┘. If you get the message *File not found*, or if no line in the file begins with the word *PATH*, your system does not have a PATH command, so proceed to Step 2. If a line in the file does begin with *PATH*, look to see if the name of your DOS directory is listed on the line. For example, if your DOS files are in a directory named DOS, one part of the line should read *C:\DOS*. If your directory is listed, you can execute DOS external commands without any concern for the directory they are stored in. The PATH command tells DOS to look for them in the listed directory.

2. If your system does not have a PATH command, you have to either be in the DOS directory to execute an external command or refer to the directory in the command. For example, to move into the DOS directory, assuming it is named DOS, type **CD \DOS** and press Enter◄┘.

THE AUTOEXEC.BAT FILE

When you boot your system, one of the first things it does is look for a file on the startup drive named AUTOEXEC.BAT. This file contains commands that are then executed before the command prompt is displayed.

►T U T O R I A L

In this tutorial, you experiment with some basic commands. (To execute the CHKDSK command described in this tutorial, you will need a copy of the DOS utility file CHKDSK.COM or CHKDSK.EXE.) If your system uses more than one DOS disk, ask which disk it is on.

GETTING STARTED

1. Load DOS so that the command prompt is displayed.
2. Insert the original write-protected copy of the *Student Resource Disk* into drive A.
3. Type **A:** and press Enter◄┘, and the command prompt indicates that drive A is the default drive.
4. Check that the printer is on and has paper in it.

EXECUTING SOME INTERNAL COMMANDS

5. Type **DATE** and press Enter◄┘ to display the current date and a prompt asking you to enter a new date.
6. Press Enter◄┘, and the date is left unchanged. The command prompt reappears.
7. Type **TIME** and press Enter◄┘ to display the current time and a prompt asking you to enter a new time.
8. Press Enter◄┘, and the time is left unchanged. The command prompt reappears.
9. Type **CLS** and press Enter◄┘ to clear the screen and move the command prompt to the upper left corner of the screen.

LOOKING AHEAD: THE CHKDSK COMMAND

You use the CHKDSK command to find out how much space is still available on a disk and in the computer's memory. This command also tells you if all the files on your disk are stored correctly. If it finds that they are scattered, you will see a message that files are in noncontiguous blocks. This is discussed in Topic 12.

10. Type **DIR** and press Enter⏎ to list the names of the files on the disk.

EXECUTING SOME EXTERNAL COMMANDS

11. If you are working on a floppy disk system (leave things as is on a hard disk system):
    - Move the *Student Resource Disk* to drive B.
    - Type **B:** and press Enter⏎ to change the default drive to B.
    - Insert the DOS disk containing the DOS utility file CHKDSK.COM or CHKDSK.EXE into drive A. (Ask your instructor if you are not sure of which disk to use.)

12. Enter a command as follows:
    - On a hard disk system, type **CHKDSK** and press Enter⏎.
    - On a floppy disk system, type **A:CHKDSK** and press Enter⏎.

    The screen indicates how much room is on your disk and in your internal memory and how much of it has been used. If you get a message that tells you it is a bad command or filename, see the box "External Commands on Hard Disk Systems" in the introduction to this topic

13. Type **TYPE WHATSUP.DOC** and press Enter⏎. The contents of the file are scrolled up the screen too fast to read them.

14. If you are working on a floppy disk system, insert the DOS disk containing the DOS utility file MORE.COM into drive A. (It's probably on the same disk you inserted into drive A earlier.)

15. Enter a command as follows: (The | character is the split vertical bar(⋮) on the backslash (\) key. You must press ⇧ Shift to enter it.)
    - On a hard disk system, type **TYPE WHATSUP.DOC | MORE** and press Enter⏎.
    - On a floppy disk system, type **TYPE WHATSUP.DOC | A:MORE** and press Enter⏎.

    The list of Bugs Bunny films directed by Chuck Jones scrolls onto the screen until the screen is full. Then, the screen pauses, and the prompt - - *More* - - is displayed at the bottom of the screen.

16. Press any key to scroll through the document a screenful at a time until the command prompt reappears.

FINISHING UP

17. Either continue to the next activity or quit for the day. To quit, remove your disks from the drive and turn off the computer.

LOOKING AHEAD: SPECIFYING PATHS TO A PROGRAM

The CHKDSK command is an external command, so DOS needs to know where this file is located when you execute the command. If it is not on the default drive, you have to specify which drive it is on. If the file is on drive A, you indicate its location by specifying A:CHKDSK. The A: part of the command is called a path since it tells DOS what path to follow to find the file.

THE MORE COMMAND

When you display directories or files from DOS, they may scroll off the top of the screen too fast to be read. In these cases, you can use the | MORE command to pause the screen whenever the screen is full. The command then displays a message - - *More* - - and you press any key to scroll to the next screenful of data.

▶ **Q U I C K   R E F E R E N C E**

To execute commands, you type them in and press Enter⏎. However, you can also save time by executing a command you have used previously without having to retype it or by editing it into a new form.

Executing Commands

To execute commands from the command prompt, you type the name of the command and press [Enter←] When the command is finished executing, the command prompt reappears.

When you type commands, there are certain conventions that you must follow. Getting used to these conventions takes practice. If you do not follow them exactly, an error message is displayed, but no harm is done. When entering commands, keep the following conventions in mind:

- You can use uppercase, lowercase, or any combination of case. For example, when checking a disk, you can type **CHKDSK**, **chkdsk**, or **Chkdsk**, and the computer accepts them all.
- Parts of many commands must be separated from each other by *delimiters*. Delimiters, which are like punctuation marks in English, indicate where parts of a command begin or end. DOS delimiters include spaces, colons, and slashes.
  - Spaces should not be used at times. For example, you do not enter spaces between the drive, path, and filename. You type **B:**<*filename*> not **B: **<*filename*>. The colon and backslash act as the delimiters.
  - Spaces should be used at other times. For example, when displaying a directory of a disk other than the default, you type **DIR B:** not **DIRB:**.
- Many commands can include optional *switches* that modify them. These switches must be separated from the command by a delimiter. For example, to display the directory of a disk in drive B across the screen, you type **DIR B:/W**.

Responding to Prompts

When working with DOS and application programs, you often encounter prompts, which are simply requests for you to supply the computer with information it needs. Some prompts, like the command prompt, are cryptic. Others are more helpful; for example, a prompt may ask *Insert new diskette for drive A Press Enter to continue*. To enter responses to these prompts, you take the requested actions. Some commands then continue automatically. With others, you have to enter a response like **Y** or **N** (for Yes or No), and then you sometimes have to confirm that response by pressing [Enter←] to continue.

Editing Commands

When you type commands, you might make a mistake, or you might want to repeat the same command, perhaps with a few changes. DOS has editing keys and commands that allow you to do each of these things.

To cancel a command that you have not yet executed by pressing [Enter←], press [Ctrl]-[Break] or [Ctrl]-[C] (hold down [Ctrl] while you press the second key) to return to the command prompt.

When entering a command, you can press [←Bksp] to delete typos. To cancel a partially entered command, press [Esc]. This places a backslash (\\) character at the end of the current line and moves the cursor down one line ready for a new command. At this point, you can either press [Enter←] to return to the command prompt, or enter a new command and press [Enter←].

The last command you typed is stored in a buffer, a small area of memory used to store keystrokes. You can recall the command from that buffer to edit it. There are many commands you can use to do so, but the two most popular are `F1`, which displays the previous command one character at a time, and `F3`, which displays the complete command. Once the command is displayed on the command line, you can press `Enter←` to execute it or press `← Bksp` to delete characters and type new ones at the end of the line.

DOS 5 added a new feature called DOSKEY that makes it easy to repeat or edit previous commands. To use this feature, type **DOSKEY** and press `Enter←` to load this external command. Once it has been loaded, it stores each command you use so that you can redisplay any of them on the command line. To display a list of all commands that have been saved, type **DOSKEY /HISTORY** and press `Enter←` or press `F7`.

To display a specific command so that you can repeat it or edit it, press `↑` or `PgDn` to display the command you used most recently, or press `PgUp` to display the oldest command you used. Once you have displayed a command, you can use `↑` and `↓` to scroll back and forward through them.

Once the command you want is displayed on the command line, you can press `Enter←` to execute it, or you can edit it by moving the cursor through the command and inserting or deleting characters. To delete a character, you move the cursor under it, and type a new character or press `Del`. You can also move the cursor to the right of a character, and press `← Bksp` to delete it. To insert characters, press `Ins` to turn on insert mode, and the cursor should change shape to indicate that you are in insert mode. Move the cursor to where you want to insert one or more characters, and type them in. The characters above the cursor and those to its right move aside to make room for the new characters. The commands used most frequently with DOSKEY are described in the table "DOSKEY Edit Commands."

DOSKEY EDIT COMMANDS

Key	Description
`↑` or `PgDn`	Displays the command you used most recently.
`PgUp`	Displays the oldest command you used.
`↑` and `↓`	Scrolls back and forward through the displayed commands.
`←` or `→`	Moves the cursor left or right one character.
`Ctrl`-`←` or `Ctrl`-`→`	Moves the cursor left or right one word.
`Home` or `End`	Moves the cursor to the beginning or end of line.
`Esc`	Removes the command from the display.
`F7`	Displays all stored commands as a numbered list.
`Alt`-`F7`	Erases all stored commands.
`F8`	Searches for the stored command you want. Type the first few characters in the command, and press `F8` to display the most recent version you used. Press `F8` to cycle through any other versions being stored.
`F9`	Prompts you to type the number of a command you want to repeat. (Use `F7` to find numbers.)

TIP

If numbers appear when you press the arrow keys on the numeric keypad, the `NumLock` key is engaged. To disengage it, press it once.

EXERCISE 1

PRINTING THE SCREEN

In some cases, your instructor may want a printed record of the commands you execute in the activities in this text. If you are requested to submit printed results, there are two ways to do so. You can print the current screen, or you can turn on printing so that everything that appears on your screen is printed. Complete this exercise only if your instructor approves since the commands discussed here can cause problems on some systems.

1. Be sure your printer is on. If you use one of the commands in this exercise when your printer isn't on, your system may "hang" and not accept keyboard input until you turn the printer on.
2. Type **DIR/W** and press Enter⏎ to display a list of the files on the disk.
3. Press ⇧Shift-PrtScr (or just PrtScr on an enhanced keyboard) to print what is currently displayed on the screen. (To see the printout on some printers, you may have to press On Line to take the printer off line, FF for Form Feed, and then On Line again to put the printer back on line.)
4. Press Ctrl-PrtScr to turn on screen printing so that you will have a running, printed record of what you do while working from the command prompt.
5. Repeat the tutorial at the beginning of this topic. When finished, press Ctrl-PrtScr again to turn printing off.

EXERCISE 2

EXECUTING INTERNAL AND EXTERNAL COMMANDS

In this exercise, you practice executing internal and external commands. All the commands that you enter here are similar to those you entered in this topic's tutorial. If you need help on a command, refer to the tutorial to see how you executed it there.

1. Insert your disks as follows:
   - On a hard disk system, insert the *Student Resource Disk* into drive A.
   - On a floppy disk system, insert the DOS startup disk into drive A and the *Student Resource Disk* into drive B.
2. If your instructor approves, press Ctrl-PrtScr to turn on printing.
3. Change the date to January 2, 1993.
4. Change the time to 10:30 a.m.
5. Display the path if your system has one.
6. Clear the screen.
7. Use the CHKDSK command to check the disk in drive A.

8. Display a directory of the disk in drive A in five columns.

EXERCISE 3

EXPLORING DOS 5'S DOSKEY FEATURE

In this exercise, you explore DOS 5's DOSKEY feature that allows you to repeat or edit previous commands. For this feature to work, the DOSKEY program must be loaded into memory.

1. Insert your disks as follows:
   - On a hard disk system, insert the *Student Resource Disk* into drive A.
   - On a floppy disk system, insert the DOS startup disk into drive A and the *Student Resource Disk* into drive B.
2. Enter the following command:
   - On a hard disk system, type **DIR A:** and press [Enter←].
   - On a floppy disk system, type **DIR B:** and press [Enter←].
3. Press [↑] to see if it displays the previous command on the command line. If so, your DOSKEY program has been loaded. If the previous command does not appear on the command line, DOSKEY has not been loaded. To load it, type **DOSKEY** and press [Enter←]. (Immediately after it loads, a message reads *DOSKey installed*. If this message doesn't appear, ask your instructor for help.)
4. If DOSKEY is operating correctly on your system, repeat Exercise 1. Then repeat it again, but this time press [↑] until any command you want is displayed on the command line (once you have scrolled up, you can also press [↓] to back down through commands), and press [Enter←] to execute it.
5. You can edit previous commands. To see how this works, display a previous command, and press [←] and [→] to move the cursor through it. Type new characters, and then press [Ins] and type some more. Before you press [Ins], characters you type replace any character in the cursor's position. After pressing it, new characters are inserted and text to the right is pushed aside. Use [Del] and [← Bksp] to delete characters. To cancel the command without executing it, press [Ctrl]-[C].

DOS EXTERNAL COMMAND FILES

File	Disk
CHKDSK	_____
COMP	_____
DOSKEY	_____
FORMAT	_____
LABEL	_____
MORE	_____
PRINT	_____
SORT	_____
SYS	_____
TREE	_____
TYPE	_____
XCOPY	_____

EXERCISE 4

LOCATING DOS FILES NEEDED FOR EXTERNAL COMMANDS

When you execute an external command, the DOS file for that command must be on a disk in one of the disk drives. If you are working on a floppy disk system that has more than one DOS disk, locate the disks that contain the files listed in the table "DOS External Command Files." The files will have the name shown in the table, but their extensions may be either .EXE or .COM. To locate the files, put each DOS disk into drive A one at a time, type **DIR A:** and press [Enter←] to list the files on the disk. If the filenames scroll by too fast to read, type **DIR A:/W** and press [Enter←].

■ ■ ■ ■ ■ ■ ■ ■ ■

Changing the Default Drive

After completing this topic, you will be able to:
- Describe the difference between the default drive and other drives
- Change default drives
- Customize the command prompt

When you first turn on your computer to boot the system, drive A spins. If a disk in that drive contains the necessary operating system files, the operating system is loaded. Drive A operates because the computer's designers have placed a program in the computer's ROM telling it that it should address this drive when first turned on. Since it addresses drive A automatically, drive A is the default startup drive. (On a hard disk system, it then looks to drive C if no disk is in drive A.)

Although you cannot change the default drive that the computer addresses when you first turn it on, you can, and often do, copy, rename, delete, and save files on a drive other than the default drive. To do so, you can change the default drive.

The Default Drive
The default drive is the drive your computer automatically addresses when you execute commands. It's like a model railroad where you can set a switch to send a train down one track or another.

Changing the Default Drive
You can change the default drive so that the program automatically addresses another drive. It's like changing the position of the switch on a model railroad to send the train down another track.

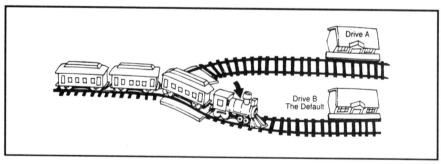

In this tutorial, you change the default drive.

GETTING STARTED

1. Load DOS so that the command prompt is displayed.
2. Insert your disks as follows:
   - On a hard disk system, insert the *Student Resource Disk* into drive A.
   - On a floppy disk system, insert the DOS disk into drive A and the *Student Resource Disk* into drive B.

CHANGING THE COMMAND PROMPT

3. Type **PROMPT What can I do for you?** and press Enter ⏎ to change the prompt. Changes in the prompt stay in effect until you turn off the computer unless you use the PROMPT command again to change it.
4. Type **PROMPT PG** and press Enter ⏎. The PG at the end of the text is a DOS command that tells the computer to display the current default drive, in this case, *C:\>* or *A:\>*.
5. Type **PROMPT The default drive is now PG** and press Enter ⏎ to have the prompt indicate the current default drive as you complete the steps that follow.

CHANGING THE DEFAULT DRIVE

6. Enter the command as follows:
   - On a hard disk system, type **C:** and press Enter ⏎.
   - On a floppy disk system, type **B:** and press Enter ⏎.

   When you enter this command, the command prompt changes to indicate the current default drive.
7. Type **DIR** and press Enter ⏎ to display a list of files on the current default drive.
8. Type **A:** and press Enter ⏎ to change the default drive to A.
9. Type **DIR** and press Enter ⏎ to display a list of files on the new default drive.
10. Enter the command as follows:
    - On a hard disk system, type **C:** and press Enter ⏎.
    - On a floppy disk system, type **B:** and press Enter ⏎.
11. Type **A:** and press Enter ⏎.

FINISHING UP

12. Type **PROMPT PG** and press Enter ⏎ to have the prompt indicate the default drive without the preceding text.
13. Either continue to the next activity or quit for the day. To quit, remove your disks from the drives and turn off the computer.

When working with DOS and application programs, you need to change the default drive. At times, it is helpful to customize the command prompt so that it provides you with information that you need.

Changing the Default Drive

To change the default drive from the command prompt, type the letter of the drive and a colon and press [Enter←]. For example, if the default drive is set to A and you want to change it to B, type **B:** and press [Enter←]. The command prompt is usually set to indicate the current default drive. For example, *B>* or *B:\>* indicates that drive B is the default drive.

In a system with a single floppy disk drive, the drive functions as both drive A and drive B. If the command prompt reads *A>* and you type **B:** and press [Enter←], the command prompt changes to *B>*. On such systems, when you execute DOS commands such as copying files from one disk to another, you are frequently asked to swap disks in the drive.

Changing the Command Prompt

The default command prompt (which you get if you type **PROMPT** and press [Enter←]) is the letter of the current default drive followed by a greater-than sign, but you can customize the prompt to display other useful information. To change the command prompt, you can use any of the commands, either alone or in combination, described in the table "Prompt Commands." Note that each of these commands is preceded by a dollar sign so that it will not be treated as text and appear just as typed. The prompt command **PROMPT PG** is probably the most frequently used version. It displays the current drive (and directory, as you will see later).

PROMPT COMMANDS

Character	Description
$_	Inserts a carriage return and line feed when you want to create two or more lines on the prompt; for example, **PROMPT TIME = T_DATE = D_PG** displays the time on one line, the date on the next, and the current drive and directory on the third.
$B	Displays a I (split vertical bar).
$D	Displays the current date.
$E	Displays an ← (Esc) character.
$G	Displays a > (greater-than) character.
$H	Backspace that deletes the previous character in the prompt.
$L	Displays a < (less-than) character.
$N	Displays the default drive.
$P	Displays the current directory of the default drive. (If you use this character on a floppy disk system, the disk drive must always have a disk in it when you make it the default drive; otherwise, you get the error message *Not ready reading drive x*. (The *x* is the specified drive and varies depending on the system you are using.) If this prompt appears, press [F] (for *Fail*) to continue.
$Q	Displays an equal sign (=).

PROMPT COMMANDS (CONTINUED)

Character	Description
$T	Displays the current time.
$V	Displays the DOS version number.
$<spaces>	Type **$** and then press Spacebar to insert spaces. If you insert a space after the last character in the PROMPT command, the cursor will be spaced one character to the right of the prompt.

> **E X E R C I S E**

EXERCISE 1

CHANGING BETWEEN DRIVES A AND B ON A SYSTEM WITH A SINGLE FLOPPY DISK DRIVE

If your system has only a single floppy disk drive, you can explore how it acts as both drive A and drive B. You will find this feature very useful when you want to copy files between disks in later tutorials and in your own work. As you complete the following steps, watch the prompts that appear on the screen; then press Enter ↵ to remove them before proceeding to the next step. Whenever you see the prompt asking you to insert a disk, you can remove one disk and then insert another before continuing. This way you can use the single drive in your system as though it were two separate drives.

1. Load DOS.
2. Insert your *Student Resource Disk* into drive A.
3. Type **A:** and press Enter ↵ so that the command prompt *A>* or *A:\>* is displayed.
4. Type **B:** and press Enter ↵.
5. Type **A:** and press Enter ↵.
6. Type **DIR B:** and press Enter ↵.
7. Type **DIR A:** and press Enter ↵.

REVIEW

- Loading the operating system is called booting the system. If the computer is off, it is called a cold boot. If the system is already on, it is called a warm boot.
- When you load DOS, either the command prompt or the DOS Shell is displayed, depending on which version of DOS you're using and how your system has been set up.
- DOS has internal and external commands. The internal commands are part of the COMMAND.COM file and are always available whenever the command prompt is displayed on the screen. External commands are stored in their own files. To use one of them, the file must be on a disk in one of the drives.
- The default drive is the drive that the computer addresses unless you specify another drive. To change the default drive, you type its letter and a colon and press [Enter ←].

QUESTIONS

FILL IN THE BLANK

1. If you make a typo when typing a command, you can press _____ to delete it.
2. After typing a command, you press _____ to send it to the CPU.
3. The *A>*, *A:\>*, *C>*, *C:\>* or something similar that appears on the screen when you boot your system is called the _____ _____.
4. To enter the date January 10, 1994, into a computer, you would type _____.
5. To enter the time ten-thirty a.m. into a computer, you would type _____.
6. To warm-boot many computers, you hold down _____ and _____ and then press _____.
7. To find out what version of DOS is in your computer's memory, you use the _____ command.
8. Commands that are always available when the command prompt is on the screen are called _____ commands.
9. Commands that are available only when the file that contains them is on a disk in one of the disk drives are called _____ commands.
10. To repeat the previous command, you press _____ and then press _____.
11. To print the text currently on the screen, you would press _____.

12. To print all text that will appear on the screen with subsequent commands, you would press _____.
13. To change the way the command prompt looks, you use the _____ command.
14. To change the default drive from drive A to drive B, you type _____ and press _____.
15. To change the default drive from drive B to drive A, you type _____ and press _____.

MATCH THE COLUMNS

1. VER
2. F3
3. Ctrl - Alt - Del
4. ← Bksp
5. Prompts
6. ⇧ Shift - PrtScr or PrtScr
7. Ctrl - PrtScr
8. PROMPT
9. A> or A:\>
10. A: and then Enter ←
11. B: and then Enter ←

___ Repeats the previous command
___ Command prompt
___ Command that customizes the command prompt
___ Changes the default drive to drive A
___ Computer's request for you to type something
___ Prints all screen text until you turn it off
___ Prints text currently on the screen
___ Deletes typos when entering commands
___ Keys you press to warm-boot many computers
___ Changes the default drive to drive B
___ The command that tells you what version of DOS is in memory

WRITE OUT THE ANSWER

1. What does booting a computer mean?
2. What is the startup drive? Which drive is it on a floppy disk system? On a hard disk system?
3. What is the difference between a warm boot and a cold boot? How do you do each?
4. What is the basic difference between an internal and an external DOS command?
5. Name and describe the use of three function keys that can be used with DOS.
6. What is the default drive? Describe how you change it.
7. What does the A> prompt mean? The B> prompt?

PROJECTS

PROJECT 1

VIEWING A VIDEO

Many videocassettes have been developed to introduce users to specific operating systems. Visit your library, learning center, and computer lab to see if any are available for you to view. If there are, view one, and then summarize its key points.

PROJECT 2

CREATING A DOS REFERENCE CARD

The table "Summary of DOS Commands" lists some of the most frequently used DOS command procedures. Complete the table by entering in the Command column the command you would use to perform each of the tasks. In the Type column, indicate if the command is an internal or external command.

SUMMARY OF DOS COMMANDS

Description	Command	Type
Basic Commands		
Displays DOS version number	_____	_____
Displays system date	_____	_____
Displays system time	_____	_____
Changes the command prompt	_____	_____
Clears the screen	_____	_____
Changing Default Drives		
Makes drive A the default drive	_____	_____
Makes drive B the default drive	_____	_____
Makes drive C the default drive	_____	_____

Basic DOS Utilities

Formatting Disks

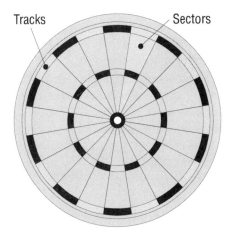

Tracks   Sectors

A Formatted Disk

One way to visualize a formatted disk is as a dart board. Tracks run in circles around the disk. The number of tracks per inch determines the density of the disk. A high-density disk has more tracks per inch than a low-density disk and can therefore store more data. Since the tracks can store a great deal of data, the computer divides them into sectors, which makes it easier to find a location on the disk. These sectors are like pie-shaped wedges that radiate from the center of the disk.

After completing this topic, you will be able to:

■ Describe why you format a disk and what happens when you do
■ Format your own data disks
■ Explain the difference between a data disk and a system disk
■ Format a disk as a system disk
■ Transfer the operating system files to a disk that has already been formatted

When you open a box of new floppy disks, they will usually not work properly on your computer because they have been designed to work with a variety of computer systems. To customize them so that they will work with the equipment you are using, you format the disks. Formatting checks the disk surface for unusable spots, divides the disk into tracks and sectors, and creates a directory.

Formatting a disk effectively erases any data that may already have been saved on it. You therefore have to be careful with this command. You should never format a previously used disk unless you are sure you will not need any of the files on it. Moreover, you should never format a hard disk drive unless you are willing to lose every file on the disk. However, since no one is perfect and mistakes do happen, DOS 5 added an unformat command that helps you recover files should you format a disk by mistake.

▶ TUTORIAL

(your name)
Resource Disk—Backup
Formatted with DOS (version number)

The Resource Disk—Backup Label

In this tutorial, you format a blank data disk for use in the tutorials and exercises in this text.

GETTING STARTED

1. Load DOS so that the command prompt is displayed.
2. Label a blank disk, using as a guide the information shown in the figure "The Resource Disk—Backup Label."
3. Insert your disks as follows:
   ■ On a hard disk system, insert the disk labeled *Resource Disk—*

Backup into drive A.

- On a floppy disk system, insert the DOS disk that contains the file FORMAT.COM into drive A and the disk labeled *Resource Disk—Backup* into drive B.

4. Set your drives as follows:
   - On a hard disk system, change the default drive to drive C.
   - On a floppy disk system, change the default drive to drive A.

FORMATTING A DATA DISK

5. Enter the command as follows:
   - On a hard disk system, type **FORMAT A:** and press [Enter←].
   - On a floppy disk system, type **FORMAT B:** and press [Enter←].

   In a moment, a prompt asks you to insert a disk into the drive you entered in the FORMAT command and press or strike [Enter←] when ready. You already inserted the disks in Step 3.

6. Press [Enter←] and the drive spins as it formats the disk.
   - On DOS 4 and later versions, a message is displayed on the screen to keep you posted on the progress. When the message reads *Format complete*, the drive stops.
   - If you are using DOS 4 or later, you are prompted to enter a volume label. Type your last name (abbreviate to 11 characters if necessary), and press [Enter←] to continue.

7. When the prompt reads *Format another (Y/N)?*, press [N] and then [Enter←].

   Information is displayed on the screen about the disk's status. The information varies slightly between DOS 3 and later versions but includes the following:
   - The number of bytes of total disk space and how many bytes are currently available. Usually the two numbers are the same; if they are different, DOS may have found bad sectors on the disk. If it did, it marked them so that no data can be stored on them.
   - The number of bytes in each allocation unit and the number of allocation units are displayed on DOS 4 and later versions.
   - The volume's serial number is displayed on DOS 4 and later versions.

FINISHING UP

8. You have now completed this tutorial. Either continue to the next activity or quit for the day.

QUICK REFERENCE

To format a data disk, you use the FORMAT command. The FORMAT.COM file must be on one of the drives since this is an external command.

DOS always formats a disk to match the drive it is being formatted in unless you specify otherwise. To change the way a disk is formatted, you add switches to the FORMAT command to control the formatting

LOOKING AHEAD: SWITCHES

Many DOS commands have options you can specify to control or vary the results of the command. To tell DOS to use these options, you add switches to the command. Most switches are specified by typing a slash followed by a letter or number. For example, to format a disk you might use command FORMAT /4 instead of simply FORMAT.

process. For example, you may want to format a 360KB disk in a 1.2MB drive or a 720KB 3½-inch disk in a 1.44MB drive. To format a 360KB disk in a 1.2MB 5¼-inch drive, use the command FORMAT *<drive:>* / 4. To format a 720KB disk in a 1.44MB 3½-inch drive, use the command FORMAT *<drive:>* /T:80 /N:9 (or FORMAT *<drive:>* /F:720 on versions 4.0 and later).

→ **K E Y / S t r o k e s**

Formatting Floppy Disks

1. Insert your disks as follows:
   - On a hard disk system, insert the disk to be formatted into drive A.
   - On a floppy disk system, insert the disk with the file FORMAT.COM into drive A and the disk to be formatted into drive B.
2. Set your drives as follows:
   - On a hard disk system, make drive C the default drive.
   - On a floppy disk system, make drive A the default drive.
3. Enter the command as follows:
   - On a hard disk system, type **FORMAT A:** and press [Enter ←].
   - On a floppy disk system, type **FORMAT B:** and press [Enter ←].

   In a moment, a prompt asks you to insert a disk into the drive you entered in the FORMAT command and press or strike [Enter ←] when ready. You inserted the disks in Step 1.
4. Press [Enter ←] to continue and the drive spins as it formats the disk. On DOS 4 and later versions, a message is displayed on the screen to keep you posted on the progress. (DOS 5 also saves UNFORMAT information.) When the message reads *Format complete*, the drive stops.

   If you are using DOS 4 or later, a prompt reads *Volume label (11 characters, ENTER for none)?*. Either type a volume name to identify the disk and press [Enter ←] or press [Enter ←] without entering a volume name.

   The prompt reads *Format another (Y/N)?*.
5. Either: Press [N] and then [Enter ←] to quit formatting and return to the command prompt.

   Or: Insert a new disk into the same drive as you did in Step 1, press [Y] and then [Enter ←] to display the prompt asking you to insert a new disk. Press the designated key to continue.

Creating System Disks

When you boot the computer, it looks in the startup drive for the file COMMAND.COM and two hidden system files named IBMBIO.COM and IBMDOS.COM (or something similar on some versions of DOS). The DOS startup disk contains these files, but you can also put them onto your own floppy disks, which are then called system disks because they can be used to boot the system.

■   ■   ■   ■   ■   ■   ■   ■   ■

There are two ways to transfer these files to your own floppy disk: either during or after formatting.

- To transfer the files during formatting, add the /S switch to the FORMAT command. For example, to format a disk on drive A as a system disk, type **FORMAT A: /S** and press Enter ⏎ . On most systems this switch copies the two hidden system system files and the file COMMAND.COM to the floppy disk. On some systems, however, it does not copy COMMAND.COM and you must copy it separately with the COPY command. (See the box "Copying COMMAND.COM.")

- If there is room for them on an already formatted floppy disk, you can transfer the two hidden system files to it with the external command SYS. For example, to transfer the system files to an already formatted disk in drive A, type **SYS A:** and press Enter ⏎ . The SYS command does not copy the file COMMAND.COM. You have to copy it separately with the COPY command. (See the box "Copying COMMAND.COM.")

LOOKING AHEAD: COPYING COMMAND.COM

You will learn about copying files in Topic 6. For now, just follow these directions to copy COMMAND.COM to a floppy disk.

1. Insert the DOS startup disk into drive A.
2. Insert the formatted system disk into drive B.
3. Make drive A the default drive by typing **A:** and pressing Enter ⏎ .
4. Type **COPY COMMAND. COM B:** and press Enter ⏎ .

Unformatting a Disk

If you format a disk by mistake, you can lose valuable files because the FORMAT command erases them. For this reason, many companies have published special programs you can use to restore deleted files. With the introduction of DOS 5, an UNFORMAT external command was added so that you can use DOS to unformat a disk and restore the lost files. To unformat a disk, type **UNFORMAT** <*drive*> and press Enter ⏎ . For example, to unformat a disk in drive A, type **UNFORMAT A:** and press Enter ⏎ .

To ensure that this command works, you should load DOS 5's Mirror program before formatting a disk. This program saves data that can be used to unformat the disk (specifically the file allocation table and the root directory) in a file named MIRROR.FIL. To load the Mirror program, type **MIRROR** <*drive*> and press Enter ⏎ . To mirror more than one drive, list each drive after the command. For example, to mirror drives A and C, type **MIRROR A: C:** and press Enter ⏎ . The UNFORMAT command may work on a disk that was formatted without MIRROR loaded, but your risks of not being successful increase, and the process takes longer. Moreover, for the most likelihood of success, unformat the disk immediately. If you save any files on it, they may overwrite files from the previous format, and the overwritten files will not be recoverable.

Selecting Floppy Disks for Your System

When you format a disk, the operating system divides it into tracks and sectors, an invisible magnetic pattern something like a dart board. On a formatted disk, tracks run in circles around the disk. Because tracks can store a great deal of data, the computer needs to divide them into sectors, which makes it easier to find a location on the disk. These sectors are like pie-shaped wedges that divide each track into the same number of sectors.

On early computers, disks were single-sided. All disks used now are double-sided. To store more data, the tracks on the disk are placed closer together. The spacing of these tracks is measured as tracks per inch (TPI). The number of TPI determines the density of the disk and the amount of data that can be stored on it. A high-density disk has more tracks per inch than a low-density disk and can therefore store more data. The maximum density that can be used to store data on a disk is indicated on the disk label and box. For example, on 5¼-inch disks:

- Double-density disks can store data on 48 TPI or up to 360KB.
- High-density disks (also called high-capacity or quad-density disks) can store data on 96 TPI or up to 1.2MB.

The smaller 3½-inch floppy disks can store 720KB or 1.44MB. These disks can store more data than the larger 5¼-inch disks because they can store data on 135 TPI. You can tell the two types of disks apart as follows:

- A 720KB disk is labeled 1.0MB or 2HC and has a single square cutout.
- A 1.44MB disk is labeled 2.0MB or HD and has two square cutouts.

Because of these variations in the way computers assign tracks and sectors, the disks you use must be appropriate for your system. Some of the possible combinations are shown in the tables "Formatting and Reading 5¼-Inch Disks" and "Formatting and Reading 3½-Inch Disks."

FORMATTING AND READING 5¼-INCH DISKS

Procedure	360KB Drive	1.2MB Drive
Format a 360KB disk	Yes	Yes*
Format a 1.2MB disk	No	Yes
Read a 360KB disk	Yes	Yes
Read a 1.2MB disk	No	Yes

With switches

FORMATTING AND READING 3½-INCH DISKS

Procedure	720KB Drive	1.44MB Drive
Format a 720KB disk	Yes	Yes*
Format a 1.44MB disk	No	Yes
Read a 720KB disk	Yes	Yes
Read a 1.44MB disk	No	Yes

With switches

Volume Labels

It can be useful to give your disks a label (name) that will appear on the screen whenever you look at their directory or use the VOL command. When you format a disk, DOS 4 and later versions automatically prompt you to enter a volume label. On earlier versions, you can add a label by using the command **FORMAT B: /V**. You can also add or change a label after a disk has been formatted with the LABEL command (an external command).

→ **K E Y / S t r o k e s**

Labeling a Formatted Disk

1. Insert your disks as follows:
   - On a hard disk system, make drive C the default drive.
   - On a floppy disk system, insert the disk with the LABEL.COM or LABEL.EXE file into drive A and the disk to be labeled into drive B. Make drive A the default drive.
2. Enter a command as follows:
   - On a hard disk system, type **LABEL A:** and press [Enter←].
   - On a floppy disk system, type **LABEL B:** and press [Enter←].
   A prompt reads *Volume label (11 characters, ENTER for none)?*.
3. Type a new label, and press [Enter←].

EXERCISE 1

FORMATTING ADDITIONAL DATA DISKS

Format any additional data disks that you might need for your own work.

EXERCISE 2

ADDING A VOLUME NAME

If you are using a version of DOS earlier than DOS 4, you were not prompted to enter a volume label when you formatted the *Resource Disk—Backup* in the tutorial. Use the LABEL command to label this disk with your last name (if necessary, abbreviate to 11 characters).

EXERCISE 3

CHECKING VOLUME NAMES

Use the VOL command to display the volume names for each of your floppy disks. If you find any disk with a name, write it down.

EXERCISE 4

SPECIFYING YOUR SYSTEM'S DISKS

List the specifications for the disks your system requires in the table "Disk Specifications." You will find this information in the manual that accompanies the computer. Look up "disks" or "disk drives" in the index, and refer to the listed sections. If you cannot find the information in the manual, refer to the specifications printed on the box that your disks came in.

DISK SPECIFICATIONS

Specification	Your System's Disks
Size	_____
Sides	_____
Density	_____
TPI	_____

Assigning and Listing Filenames

The file's name can have
up to eight characters

The file's extension must begin
with a period and can have up
to three characters

Filenames
Filenames have two parts: the file's name and
an optional three-character extension separated
from the file's name with a period.

After completing this topic, you will be able to:
- Describe the number and types of the characters that you can use when naming files
- List the names of files on a disk
- Use switches to modify a basic command
- Describe the function of the question mark and asterisk wildcards
- Use wildcards to specify files in commands

Character	Example
Letters	A - Z
Letters	a - z
Numbers	0 - 9
Underscore	_
Caret	^
Dollar sign	$
Tilde	~
Exclamation point	!
Number sign	#
Percent sign	%
Ampersand	&
Hyphen	-
Braces	{ }
Parentheses	( )
At sign	@
Grave accent	`
Apostrophe	'

Legal Filename Characters
You can use any of the characters shown here in
your files' names and extensions. You can type
filenames in uppercase letters, lowercase letters,
or a combination of uppercase and lowercase. If
you enter lowercase letters, the computer
automatically converts them to uppercase.

The files for the application programs you use have already been assigned names. When you use these programs to create and save your own work, you must assign names to your files. With DOS, you can assign names to files that have up to eight characters and an optional extension of up to three characters separated from the name by a period.

File Names
The characters that you can use in a filename are called *legal characters* and are shown in the figure "Legal Filename Characters." Using any other character results in a name the computer will not accept.

Each filename you use must be unique. If you assign a file the same name and extension as a file that is already on the disk, the new file will overwrite the previous file and erase it. However, you can use the same name with different extensions—for example, LETTER.DOC and LETTER.BAK. You can also use the same extension with different names.

Filename Extensions
Many application programs automatically enter extensions that identify files that they create. For example, Lotus 1-2-3 adds extensions such as .WK1 or .PIC to files it creates. dBASE adds extensions such as .DBF and .NDX. Conventions also dictate that some extensions are to be used only in specific situations. For instance, .EXE and .COM are normally used for program files, and .BAT is used for batch files. The extension .SYS is used for files containing information about your system's hardware. In many cases, if you don't use the extension the program automatically adds, the program will not be able to identify the file as its own. This can cause problems when you want to retrieve a file later.

Listing Files
Since a disk can hold many files, it is often necessary to find out what files are on a particular disk. The names of the files on a disk are held

in a directory, which you display with the DIR command. When you use this command, you control which files are listed and how they are listed using wildcards and switches. A wildcard is simply a character that stands for one or more other characters, much like a wildcard in a card game. DOS wildcards are the question mark (?) and the asterisk (*). A switch is an add-on to a command that modifies the command's performance. For example, you can use a switch to list filenames across the screen instead of down it, or to sort the listing by name, extension, date, or size.

▶ T U T O R I A L

In this tutorial, you list filenames with the DIR command and explore both wildcards and switches. Study carefully how wildcards are used. Although you are introduced to wildcards in this tutorial on the DIR command, keep in mind that they can be used with many DOS commands and with many application programs.

GETTING STARTED

1. Load DOS so that the command prompt is displayed.
2. Insert your disks as follows:
   - On a hard disk system, insert the *Student Resource Disk* into drive A.
   - On a floppy disk system, insert the DOS disk into drive A and the *Student Resource Disk* into drive B.
3. Set your drives as follows:
   - On a hard disk system, make drive A the default drive.
   - On a floppy disk system, make drive B the default drive.
4. Type **CD\DOS** and press [Enter ◄┘] to move to the DOS directory.

DISPLAYING A LIST OF FILENAMES

5. Type **DIR** and press [Enter ◄┘] to list all the files in the DOS directory on the *Student Resource Disk*.
6. List the files on the disk in another drive as follows:
   - On a hard disk system, type **DIR C:** and press [Enter ◄┘].
   - On a floppy disk system, type **DIR A:** and press [Enter ◄┘].
   Note how the periods between the files' names and extensions have been replaced with spaces.

USING THE /W SWITCH TO DISPLAY THE FILENAMES HORIZONTALLY

7. Type **DIR/W** and press [Enter ◄┘] to list the files on the default drive in five columns. The /W switch lists the files on the *Student Resource Disk* in five columns. To make room for the new columns of filenames, the size, date, and time have been dropped.
8. Display the files on the other drive in the same way:
   - On a hard disk system, type **DIR C:/W** and press [Enter ◄┘].
   - On a floppy disk system, type **DIR A:/W** and press [Enter ◄┘].

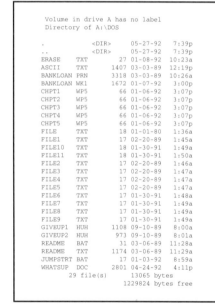

```
Volume in drive A has no label
Directory of A:\DOS

.              <DIR>      05-27-92   7:39p
..             <DIR>      05-27-92   7:39p
ERASE    TXT       27  01-08-92  10:23a
ASCII    TXT     1407  03-03-89  12:19p
BANKLOAN PRN     3318  03-03-89  10:26a
BANKLOAN WK1     1672  01-07-92   3:00p
CHPT1    WP5       66  01-06-92   3:07p
CHPT2    WP5       66  01-06-92   3:07p
CHPT3    WP5       66  01-06-92   3:07p
CHPT4    WP5       66  01-06-92   3:07p
CHPT5    WP5       66  01-06-92   3:07p
FILE     TXT       18  01-01-80   1:36a
FILE1    TXT       17  02-20-89   1:45a
FILE10   TXT       18  01-30-91   1:49a
FILE11   TXT       18  01-30-91   1:50a
FILE2    TXT       17  02-20-89   1:46a
FILE3    TXT       17  02-20-89   1:47a
FILE4    TXT       17  02-20-89   1:47a
FILE5    TXT       17  02-20-89   1:47a
FILE6    TXT       17  01-30-91   1:48a
FILE7    TXT       17  01-30-91   1:49a
FILE8    TXT       17  01-30-91   1:49a
FILE9    TXT       17  01-30-91   1:49a
GIVEUP1  HUH     1108  09-10-89   8:00a
GIVEUP2  HUH      973  09-10-89   8:01a
README   BAT       31  03-06-89  11:28a
README   TXT     1174  03-06-89  11:29a
JUMPSTRT BAT       17  01-03-92   8:59a
WHATSUP  DOC     2801  04-24-92   4:11p
     29 file(s)       13065 bytes
                    1229824 bytes free
```

A Directory Displayed from the Command Prompt

Besides listing a file's name and extension, the DIR command displays the volume name, the size of each file in bytes, the date and time the file was last saved, the number of files on the disk, and how much free space is left on the disk. (Your list will be slightly different than the one shown here).

USING THE /P SWITCH TO PAUSE THE DISPLAY OF FILENAMES

9. Enter a command as follows:
   - On a hard disk system, type **DIR /P** and press [Enter↵].
   - On a floppy disk system, type **DIR /P** and press [Enter↵].

   The /P switch displays the filenames in the DOS directory on the *Student Resource Disk* until the screen is full and then pauses and displays a prompt asking you to press or strike a key to continue. Do so, and the list continues to scroll.

USING THE * WILDCARD

10. Type **DIR** and press [Enter↵] to list all the files on the default drive. (The filenames followed by <*DIR*> are subdirectories, which you will learn about later in this text.)

11. Type **DIR *.*** and press [Enter↵] to list all the files on the default drive again.

12. Type **DIR F*.*** and press [Enter↵] to list all files that begin with the letter F.

13. Type **DIR C*.*** and press [Enter↵] to list all files that begin with the letter C.

14. Type **DIR *.TXT** and press [Enter↵] to list all files with the extension *.TXT*.

15. Type **DIR *.BAK** and press [Enter↵] to list all files with the extension *.BAK*.

16. Type **DIR *.DOC** and press [Enter↵] to list all files with the extension *.DOC*.

USING THE ? WILDCARD

17. Type **DIR** and press [Enter↵] to list all the files on the default drive again.

18. Type **DIR FILE?.TXT** and press [Enter↵] to list all files that begin with *FILE*, have up to one additional character, and have the extension *.TXT*. The files with the names FILE10.TXT and FILE11.TXT are not listed.

19. Type **DIR FILE??.TXT** and press [Enter↵] to list all files that begin with *FILE*, have up to two additional characters, and have the extension *.TXT*. Now the files with the names FILE10.TXT and FILE11.TXT are listed.

20. Type **DIR CHPT?.???** and press [Enter↵] to list all files that begin with *CHPT*, have up to one additional character, and have any extension.

21. Type **DIR C*.???** and press [Enter↵] to list all files beginning with C and with any extension of three or fewer characters.

22. Type **DIR ?????.*** and press [Enter↵] to list all filenames with five or fewer characters and any extension.

23. Type **DIR F??E?.*** and press [Enter↵] to list all filenames with four or five characters that begin with F and have E as its fourth character and any extension.

24. Press [F3] and then [Enter↵] to repeat the previous command.

SORTING THE DIR LISTING

25. To list files in alphabetical order by name, enter a command as follows:
    - If you are using DOS 4 or earlier, type **DIR | SORT** and press [Enter←].
    - If you are using DOS 5 or later, type **DIR /ON** and press [Enter←].

    SORT is an external command, so if you use that command and a message tells you that it is a bad command or filename, the SORT.EXE file is not on the disk you are using. Ask your instructor which disk contains the file.

26. To list files in alphabetical order by extension, enter a command as follows:
    - If you are using DOS 4 or earlier, type **DIR SORT /+10** and press [Enter←].
    - If you are using DOS 5 or later, type **DIR /OE** and press [Enter←].

27. To list files in order by size, enter a command as follows:
    - If you are using DOS 4 or earlier, type **DIR SORT /+14** and press [Enter←].
    - If you are using DOS 5 or later, type **DIR /OS** and press [Enter←].

28. To list files in order by date, enter a command as follows:
    - If you are using DOS 4 or earlier, type **DIR SORT /+24** and press [Enter←], to sort by the month but not the year.
    - If you are using DOS 5 or later, type **DIR /OD** and press [Enter←], to sort by the month and the year.

FINISHING UP

29. You have now completed this tutorial. Either continue to the next activity or quit for the day.

▶ Q U I C K   R E F E R E N C E

The names of files on a disk are stored in a directory that you can display with the DIR command. You can control which files are listed, and how they are listed, by adding wildcards and switches to the command.

The DIR Command

In its simplest form, the DIR command displays a listing of the directory of the disk in the default drive. For example, with the *A>* command prompt on the screen:

- To list the files in drive A, type **DIR** or **DIR A:** and press [Enter←].
- To see the files in drive B, type **DIR B:** and press [Enter←].

Besides listing filenames, the DIR command also displays the size of each file in bytes, the date and time the file was last saved, and the number of files in the current directory and the amount of free space left on the disk. DOS 5 and later versions also indicate the number of bytes occupied by the files in the current directory.

Using Switches with the DIR Command

If a list of files is too long to be displayed on the screen, some of the filenames will quickly scroll up and off the top of the screen. Two commands prevent this: DIR <drive> /W and DIR <drive> /P. The /W and /P following the commands are called switches and they modify the basic command.

With DOS 5, other switches can be used to arrange ("or sort") the list by name, extension, date, or size in ascending or descending order. All switches that can be used with the DIR command are listed and described in the table "DIR Command Switches."

DIR COMMAND SWITCHES

DOS 5 Switch	DOS 4 Switch	Description
/W	/W	The /W (for Wide) switch displays five columns of filenames instead of a single vertical list. This command drops the file size, date, and time information to make room for the additional columns of filenames. Because only the filenames are displayed and they are arranged horizontally on the screen, many filenames can be displayed on the screen at one time.
/P	/P	The /P (for Pause) switch displays filenames until the screen is full. The list then pauses, and a prompt reads *Press any key to continue.* To display more filenames, simply press any key.
/ON	ISORT	Lists file names in ascending alphabetical order.
/O-N	ISORT /R	Lists file names in descending alphabetical order.
/OE	ISORT /+10	Lists file extensions in ascending alphabetical order.
/O-E	ISORT /+10 /R	Lists file extensions in descending alphabetical order.
/OS	ISORT /+14	Lists files by size from smallest to largest.
/O-S	ISORT /+14 /R	Lists files by size from largest to smallest.
/OD	ISORT /+24	Lists files by dates from newest to oldest (DOS 4 and earlier versions sort only by month, not year.)
/O-D	ISORT /+24 /R	Lists files by dates from oldest to newest (DOS 4 and earlier versions sort only by month, not year.)

The Directory Arrangement
A directory is actually arranged into 38 columns. Each section begins in its own column, which you can specify to sort the directory by that section. For example, to sort on the extension, you specify /+10. To sort on the file's size, you specify /+14.

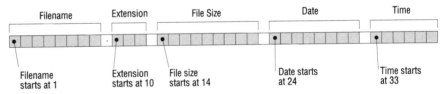

On DOS 4 and earlier versions, sorting directories is more complicated. First of all, you cannot use a sort switch with the DIR command directly. Instead, you have to use the pipe character ⌷ (the split vertical bar above the ⟨\⟩) with the SORT command and add a switch to that command as shown in the table. You then have to use a second switch to sort directories in reverse order. If you look at a directory listing carefully (see the figure "The Directory Arrangement"), you will see that each element, be it name, extension, size, or date, begins in a specific column. The numbers in the switches are the columns in which the first character of the element appears in the directory. For example, the file

Wildcards

The term *wildcard* comes from card games where a designated card, say a jack, can substitute for any other card in the deck. For example, in the card sequence 4-5-J-7-8, the jack stands for the 6 card.

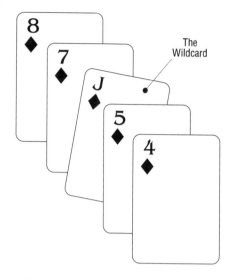

The Wildcard

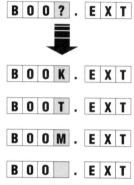

The Question Mark Wildcard

In this figure, the question mark will substitute for any character in the fourth and last position in the file's name. All other characters in filenames must be exactly as shown for a match to occur. This filename specification will therefore match files with names such as BOOK.EXT, BOOT.EXT, BOOM.EXT, and BOO.EXT.

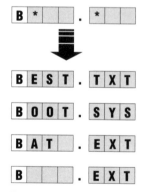

The Asterisk Wildcard

In this figure, the asterisk will substitute for all characters following the first character in the file's name and all characters in the extension. This filename specification will therefore match files beginning with the letter B that have up to eight characters in their name and any extension.

extensions are listed in the directory beginning in column 10, sizes in column 14, and dates in column 24.

Using Wildcards with the DIR Command

You use the ? and * wildcards to specify groups of files.

Using the ? Wildcard

The question mark substitutes for any single character. If you think of all filenames fitting into a grid with eight columns for the name and three columns for the extension, you can see how the question mark wildcard works.

- **????????.???** stands for the names of all files on the disk.
- **BOO?.EXT** stands for any name that has three or four characters and that begins with BOO followed by the extension .EXT.
- **BO??.EXT** stands for any name that has two to four characters and that begins with BO followed by the extension .EXT.
- **B???.???** stands for any name that has one to four characters and that begins with B followed by any extension of three or fewer characters.
- **????.E??** stands for any name that has four or fewer characters followed by any extension that begins with E.

Using the * Wildcard

The asterisk represents any character in a given position and all following characters in the part of the filename (either the name or extension) where it is used. For example, to display all filenames with the extension .DOC, type **DIR *.DOC**. Again, if you think of all filenames fitting into a grid with eight columns for the name and three columns for the extension, you can see how the asterisk wildcard works.

- ***.*** stands for any name and any extension.
- **B*.*** stands for any name that begins with B and has any extension.
- **B*.EXE** stands for any name that begins with B and has an .EXE extension.
- ***.E*** stands for any name that has an extension that begins with E.

EXERCISE 1

PRINTING DIRECTORIES

1. Turn on your printer.
2. If your instructor approves, press Ctrl-PrtScr to turn on printing.
3. Insert the *Student Resource Disk* into a floppy drive and make that drive the default drive.
4. Type **CD\DOS** and press Enter↵ to change to the DOS directory.
5. Display filenames on your original *Student Resource Disk* so that names, extensions, sizes and dates are listed.
6. Display filenames on your original *Student Resource Disk* so that just the filenames are listed in five columns.
7. Turn off printing if you turned it on.

STUDENT RESOURCE DISK FILENAME EXTENSIONS

Extension	Number
BAK	_____
BAT	_____
DOC	_____
HUH	_____
PRN	_____
TXT	_____
WK1	_____
WP5	_____

EXERCISE 2

USING WILDCARDS

1. Insert the *Student Resource Disk* into drive A and make that the default drive. Then type **CD\DOS** and press Enter↵ to change to the DOS directory.
2. Using the *.*<ext>* filename specifications, list in the table "Student Resource Disk Filename Extensions" the number of files there are with each extension. For example, to complete the first entry, type **DIR *.BAK** and press Enter↵. Then list in the table the number of filenames displayed.

Copying Files

After completing this topic, you will be able to:
- Describe the difference between the source and target drives
- Copy files from one disk to another

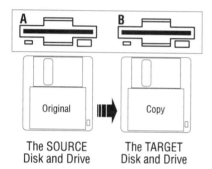

The SOURCE
Disk and Drive

The TARGET
Disk and Drive

Source and Target Drives
The source drive is the one containing the files you want to copy. The target drive is the one you want them copied to.

To copy files from one disk to another, you use the COPY command. This command is often used to make backup copies of important files. When you use this command, you usually must specify three things:

1. The drive containing the disk the files are to be copied from—the source drive unless it is the default drive.
2. The name of the files to be copied.
3. The drive containing the disk the files are to be copied to—the target drive unless it is the default drive.

Keep in mind that the source is the drive containing the disk that you want the action performed on. The target is the drive containing the disk that you want to be affected by the source. For example, to copy a file from drive A to drive B, you use the command COPY A:FILENAME.EXT B:. The A: specifies the source drive that contains the file to be copied, and the B: specifies the target drive that you want the file copied to.

If your system has only one floppy disk drive, specify the source drive as drive A and the target drive as drive B. The operating system will then prompt you to swap disks whenever it needs access to the source or target disk and it is not in the drive.

> ▶ **T U T O R I A L**

In this tutorial, you copy the files from your original *Student Resource Disk* to the disk labeled *Resource Disk—Backup* that you formatted in Topic 9.

GETTING STARTED

1. Load DOS so that the command prompt is displayed.
2. Insert your disks as follows:
   - On a hard disk system, insert the *Student Resource Disk* into drive A.
   - On a floppy disk system, insert the *Student Resource Disk* into drive A and the disk you labeled *Resource Disk—Backup* into drive B.
3. Make drive A the default drive.

COPYING A SINGLE FILE

4. Type **COPY WHATSUP.DOC B:** and press Enter ←⎮ . A message reads *1 file(s) copied*, and the command prompt reappears.

5. Type **DIR B:** and press Enter ←⎮ to see that the file was copied.

COPYING FILES USING A WILDCARD

6. Type **COPY C*.WP5 B:** and press Enter ←⎮ to copy all files beginning with the letter *C* and ending with the extension .WP5. As each file is copied, its name is listed on the screen.

7. Type **DIR B:** and press Enter ←⎮ to see that only those files beginning with the letter *C* and ending with the extension .WP5 were copied to drive B.

COPYING A FILE WITH THE TARGET DIRECTORY AS THE DEFAULT

8. Make drive B the default drive.

9. Type **COPY A:FILE1.TXT** and press Enter ←⎮ to copy the file FILE1.TXT from drive A to drive B.

10. Type **DIR** and press Enter ←⎮ to see that the file was copied to the disk in drive B even though that drive wasn't specified in the command.

COPYING ALL FILES

11. On a hard disk system, be sure the original *Student Resource Disk* is in drive A. (If your system has one floppy drive, see the box "Looking Ahead: XCOPY Command.")

12. Type **COPY A:*.* B:** and press Enter ←⎮ to copy all the files on drive A to the disk in drive B. As each file is copied, its name is listed on the screen.

13. Type **DIR B:** and press Enter ←⎮ to see that all files were copied. You have a duplicate of the *Student Resource Disk* (except for the subdirectories you will learn about later).

FINISHING UP

14. Either continue to the next activity or quit for the day.

▶ QUICK REFERENCE

The COPY command is an internal command that you can use to copy single files or groups of files. When using it, you must specify the source and target drives only if they are not the default drives. For example:

■ If the default drive is set to A, and you want to copy a file named LETTER on drive A to drive B, you would type **COPY LETTER B:**. This command reads "copy the file named LETTER in the default drive to drive B." You do not need to specify drive A because that is the default drive.

■ If the default drive is set to B, and you want to copy a file named LETTER on drive A to drive B, you would type **COPY A:LETTER**. The command reads "copy the file named LETTER in drive A to the

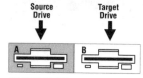

COPY FILENAME.EXT B:

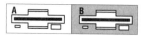

COPY A:FILENAME.EXT

COPY A:FILENAME.EXT B:

Specifying Drives in Commands

Three possible copying situations are illustrated here. In the first, the source drive is the default (shown tinted), so you need to specify only the target drive in a command. In the second, the target drive is the default, so you need to specify only the source drive in a command. In the third, neither drive is the default, so you must specify both the source and target drives in a command.

default drive." You do not need to specify drive B because that is the default drive.

■ Regardless of which drive is the default, you can specify both the source and target drives as a precaution. For example, to copy the file named LETTER from drive A to drive B regardless of which drive is the default drive, type **COPY A:LETTER B:**. This command reads "copy the file named LETTER in drive A to drive B."

If you copy a file to a disk or directory that already has a file by the same name, the copied file overwrites and replaces the original file.

→ | **K E Y / S t r o k e s**

Copying Files

1. Insert your disks as follows:
   ■ On a hard disk system, insert the source disk into drive A. You will be prompted to swap disks periodically.
   ■ On a floppy disk system, insert the source disk into drive A and the target disk into drive B.
2. Either: Type **COPY A:*.* B:** and press [Enter ←] to copy all files.
   Or: Type **COPY A:<filename.ext> B:** and press [Enter ←] to copy a single file.

▶ E X E R C I S E

EXERCISE 1

COPYING FILES

1. To copy all files with the extension .DOC from drive A to drive B, you would type _____.
2. To copy all files with the extension .TXT from drive B to drive A, you would type _____.
3. To copy all files beginning with the letter A and with the extension .DOC from drive A to drive B, you would type _____ _____.
4. To copy all files beginning with the letters CHPT followed by any single digit number (for example, CHPT1, CHPT 2, and so on) from drive A to drive B, you would type_____.

Renaming Files

There are times when you want to change the name of a file on a disk. For example, you may rename them to make your filenames consistent or to free up a name so you can use it for another file.

TUTORIALS

In this tutorial, you rename some of the files on the disk labeled *Resource Disk—Backup.* To do so, you use both the RENAME command and the shorthand version REN, which has the same effect.

Renaming Files
When you rename a file, you don't affect its contents, just the name it goes by.

GETTING STARTED

1. Load DOS so that the command prompt is displayed.
2. Insert the disk labeled *Resource Disk—Backup* into drive A, and make that the default drive.

SELECTING FILES TO BE RENAMED

3. Type **DIR CHPT *.*** and press Enter ← to display all files beginning with the letters CHPT.

RENAMING SINGLE FILES

4. Type **RENAME CHPT1.DOC CHPT6.WP5** and press Enter ← to rename the file.
5. Type **DIR *.WP5** and press Enter ← to see that the file is now listed under its new name, CHPT6.WP5, instead of its old name, CHPT1.DOC.

RENAMING GROUPS OF FILES USING WILDCARDS

6. Type **REN CHPT?.WP5 CHPT?.NEW** and press Enter ← to rename all files that begin with CHPT, have one or fewer additional letters, and end with the extension .WP5.
7. Type **DIR CHPT?.*** and press Enter ← to see that the files are listed under their original filenames but end with the extension .NEW instead of .WP5.

8. Type **REN CHPT?.NEW CHPT?.WP5** and press Enter↵ to change the names back to the way they were.

9. Type **DIR CHPT?.*** and press Enter↵ to see that the files are now listed under their original filenames.

FINISHING UP

10. Either continue to the next activity or quit for the day.

▶ Q U I C K   R E F E R E N C E

To rename files, you use the RENAME or REN command and specify both the old name and the new name for the file. You can also specify a path for the original file if it is not on the default drive. For example, to rename a file on drive A named OLDNAME.EXT to NEWNAME.EXT, you would use the command RENAME A:OLDNAME.EXT NEWNAME.EXT.

You can also use wildcards to rename groups of files. For example, to rename all files named CHPT1.WP5 through CHPT9.WP5 so that their extension becomes .DOC, you use the command REN CPTH?.WP5 CHPT?.DOC.

→ K E Y / S t r o k e s

Renaming Files

1. Select the file that you want to rename, and make the drive that it's on the default drive.

2. Type **REN** *<oldname.ext>* *<newname.ext>* and press Enter↵ .

You can also change the name of a file while copying it. For example, to copy and change the name of a file named OLDNAME.EXT, you type **COPY OLDNAME.EXT NEWNAME.EXT** and press Enter↵ .

▶ E X E R C I S E S

EXERCISE 1

RENAMING A FILE

1. Insert the disk labeled *Resource Disk—Backup* into one of the disk drives, and make that drive the default drive.

2. Use the command **REN FILE?.TXT PART?.TXT** to rename all the files that begin with FILE, have four or five characters, and end with the extension .TXT.

3. Use the DIR *.TXT command to see the results. Why were the files named FILE10.TXT and FILE11.TXT not renamed? What command would you use to change the FILE part of their name to PART?

EXERCISE 2

COPYING AND RENAMING FILES

1. Copy the file WHATSUP.DOC from the original *Student Resource Disk* to the *Resource Disk—Backup*, and change its name to MYFILE.DOC.
2. Copy the CHPT files with the extension .WP5 from and to the *Resource Disk-Backup* disk, changing their extensions to TXT as you do so. (*Hint*: You can specify the source files as CHPT?.WP5 and the target files as CHPT?.TXT to copy them in one step since they all contain five characters and only the last one varies.)

Deleting Files

After completing this topic, you will be able to:
- Preview files that will be deleted
- Delete files from a disk
- Undelete files with DOS 5 and later versions

Monitoring the amount of free space on a disk is important because many application programs misbehave when you ask them to save files on a full disk. Some programs, for example, create temporary files on your disks, and they cannot do so if the disk is too full. Most people tend to keep files long after they are useful. It is good practice to occasionally use the DIR command to list the files on a disk and then delete any of them that you no longer need.

▶ T U T O R I A L

In this tutorial, you delete files from the disk labeled *Resource Disk—Backup* using the ERASE and DEL commands.

GETTING STARTED

1. Load DOS so that the command prompt is displayed.
2. Insert the disk labeled *Resource Disk—Backup* into drive A, and make that the default drive.

PREVIEWING THE FILES TO BE DELETED

3. Type **DIR *.BAK** and press Enter⏎ to display a list of files with the extension .BAK.

DELETING A SINGLE FILE

4. Type **ERASE CHPT1.BAK** and press Enter⏎ to delete the file.
5. Type **DIR *.BAK** and press Enter⏎ to see that the file CHPT1.BAK is no longer listed in the directory.

DELETING ALL FILES WITH THE SAME EXTENSION

6. Type **DIR *.BAK** and press Enter⏎ to preview which files would be deleted using the *.BAK filename specification.
7. Type **DEL *.BAK** and press Enter⏎ to delete all files with the .BAK extension.

Deleting Files
When you delete a file, you permanently remove it from the disk and can no longer use it, (although you can recover it in some situations).

8. Type **DIR *.BAK** and press Enter⏎ to see that a message reads *File not found* since all files with the extension .BAK have been deleted.

FINISHING UP

9. Either continue to the next activity or quit for the day.

To manage your files you have to use the ERASE or DEL command to delete unneeded files. If you are using DOS 5 or later versions, you can also often recover or undelete files should you delete them by mistake.

Deleting Files

To delete one or more files, you use the ERASE or DEL command. These two internal commands are interchangeable—they work exactly alike. For example, to delete a file on drive B named FILENAME.EXT, you type either **ERASE B:FILENAME.EXT** or **DEL B:FILENAME.EXT** and press Enter⏎.

You can use wildcards with the ERASE and DEL commands, but it is dangerous to do so. Even a slight miscalculation can cause the wrong files to be deleted. However, there are precautions you can take:

■ One way to use wildcards safely is to preview what files will be affected by specifying the planned wildcards in the DIR command. If only the files you want to delete are listed, the same wildcards are safe to use with the ERASE or DEL command. For example, if you want to delete all files with the extension .BAK, type **DIR *.BAK**. If the displayed list of files can all be deleted, type **DEL *.BAK** (or type **DEL** and press F3).

■ To be prompted for each file when using DOS 4 or later, use the /P switch. For example, to delete all files with the extension .BAK, type **DEL *.BAK/P**. Before each file is deleted, a prompt reads *Delete (Y/N)?*. Press Y to delete the file, or press N to leave the file on the disk.

■ If you use the *.* wildcards, a prompt reads *Are you sure (Y/N)?*. Press Y to continue and delete all the files, or press N to cancel the command.

→ **K E Y / S t r o k e s**

Deleting Files from the Disk

1. Select the name of the file you want to delete, and make the drive that it's on the default drive.
2. Type **ERASE** *<filename>* or **DEL** *<filename>* and press Enter⏎.

Undeleting Files with DOS 5

The ERASE and DEL commands do not actually delete a file from the disk. They merely change the first letter of its name so that the name no longer appears when you display the disk's directory. This also makes the space the file occupies on the disk available for overwriting by another file. If you delete a file by mistake, do not save any files on the disk because utility programs are available that you can use to restore deleted files by putting the first letter back into their filename. One such utility program, the UNDELETE command, has been included with DOS 5 and later versions.

To undelete a file, type **UNDELETE** <*filename*> and press Enter←. For example, to undelete a file named LETTER91.WP5 on a disk in drive A, type **UNDELETE A:/LETTER91.WP5** and press Enter←. You can also use wildcards to undelete groups of files. For example, to undelete all files with the extension .WK1 of drive B, type **UNDELETE A:/*.WK1** and press Enter←. If you are not using the Mirror program to track deletions (see below), you are prompted to enter the first character in the file's name. You can also use the /ALL switch to undelete all files. If you use this switch and are not using the Mirror program to track deletions, the number sign (#) is used as the first character in each file's name. You can then use the REN command to rename the files.

To ensure that the UNDELETE command works, you should use the command MIRROR /T<*drive*> to store data about files that have been deleted. For example, to store data that can be used to undelete files on drive A, type **MIRROR /TA** and press Enter←. To mirror more than one drive, list each drive after the command. For example, to mirror drives A and C, type **MIRROR /TA /TC** and press Enter←. The first time you delete a file after loading this program, a file named PCTRACKR.DEL is created in the root directory of the drive. This file contains data that can be used to undelete files. As you delete additional files, information about them is added to the PCTRACKR.DEL file. With deletion tracking on, you can display a list of deleted files with the /LIST switch. For example, to list all deleted files on drive A, type **UNDELETE A: /LIST** and press Enter←.

The UNDELETE command may work without the Mirror program tracking deletions, but your risks of not being successful increase and you have to enter the first letter of each filename when prompted to do so. Moreover, for the highest degree of success, undelete the files immediately.

►EXERCISES

EXERCISE 1

COPYING AND THEN DELETING FILES

1. Insert the disk labeled *Resource Disk—Backup* into one of the disk drives.
2. Copy and rename all CHPT?.WP5 files to CHPT?.BAK files.
3. Delete the CHPT?.BAK files.

EXERCISE 2

DELETING A FILE

1. Insert the disk labeled *Resource Disk—Backup* into one of the disk drives.
2. Delete the ERASE.TXT file if it is on the disk.

EXERCISE 3

UNDELETING FILES WITH DOS 5

1. Insert the disk labeled *Resource Disk—Backup* into one of the disk drives.
2. Use the /LIST switch to list all deleted files.
3. Undelete one of the files.

REVIEW

- To use a new disk on your computer, you must first format it with the FORMAT command. This is an external command.
- To specify a drive other than the default, you must enter its address in the command. To display a directory of the files on the default drive, you type **DIR** and press [Enter←]. To display them on drive B when that is not the default drive, you type **DIR B:** and press [Enter←].
- Filenames on DOS computers can have eight characters followed by an extension of up to three characters (separated from the filename by a period).
- To specify more than one filename in a command on DOS computers, you use wildcards. The question mark wildcard stands for any character in the position you enter it. The asterisk wildcard stands for any character in the position you enter it and all the characters that follow up to the end of either the filename or the extension.
- The command you use to list the files on a disk is DIR, which is an internal command. You can add switches to the DIR command. DIR/W displays filenames across the screen, and DIR/P displays a screenful of names and then stops.
- The command you use to copy files is COPY, an internal command. You can use wildcards to copy groups of files. For example, COPY A:*.* B: copies all files on the disk in drive A to the disk in drive B.
- The command you use to erase files is ERASE or DEL, both of which are internal commands.
- The command you use to rename a file is RENAME (or REN), which is an internal command.

QUESTIONS

FILL IN THE BLANK

1. To prepare a disk for use on your system the first time, you usually must _____ it.
2. The command you would use to format a disk on drive B is _____.
3. DOS filenames can have up to _____ characters and an optional _____-character-long extension.
4. To list the files on a disk in drive B, you would use the command _____.
5. To list the files on a disk in drive B so that the screen display pauses when it is full, you would use the command _____.
6. To list the files on a disk in drive B in five columns, you would use the command _____.

7. To list all files with the extension .DOC on a disk in drive A, you would use the command _____.

8. To list all files with the filename LETTER and any extension on a disk in drive A, you would use the command _____.

9. To sort a directory listing of drive B by filename extension, you would enter the command _____.

10. To copy a file named REPORT.WK1 from a disk in drive A to a disk in drive B when neither drive is the default, you would use the command _____.

11. To copy a file named REPORT.WK1 from a disk in drive A to a disk in drive B when drive A is the default, you would use the command

    _____.

12. To copy all files from a disk in drive B to a disk in drive A, you would use the command _____.

13. To change the name of a file on drive A from OLDFILE.TXT to NEWFILE.DOC, you would use the command _____.

14. To delete a file named OLD.TXT from a disk in drive A, you would use the command _____.

MATCH THE COLUMNS

1. FORMAT
2. FORMAT/S
3. DIR
4. /P
5. /W
6. *
7. ?
8. COPY
9. COPY *.*
10. RENAME
11. ERASE

___ A switch added to the DIR command to pause the screen when it is full

___ A wildcard that stands for a single character

___ Changes the name of a file

___ Command used to copy files

___ Displays a list of files on the disk

___ Formats a disk as a system disk

___ Erases specified files

___ A switch added to the DIR command to display filenames in five columns

___ A wildcard that stands for more than one character

___ Command that copies all files

___ Prepares a disk so that you can store data on it

WRITE OUT THE ANSWERS

1. What is the difference between a system disk and a data disk?

2. What are the two parts of a filename called? How many characters are allowed for each part? What are the parts separated with?

3. What switch do you use to display filenames horizontally across the screen? What switch do you use to display filenames one page at a time?

4. What are wildcards used for? What two wildcards are used with DOS? Describe what each does.

5. If you are using commands that erase or copy files, how can you preview the results the commands will have?

6. When the default drive is set to A, what command do you enter to copy a file named FILENAME.EXT from drive A to drive B?

7. When the default drive is set to A, what command do you enter to copy a file named FILENAME.EXT from drive B to drive A?

8. What command do you use to rename a file? Is this command internal or external?

9. Can you rename a file while copying it? If so, how?

10. What command do you use to delete files?

11. Why must you be careful when using wildcards to delete files?

12. When using wildcards to delete groups of files, how can you preview the names of the files to be deleted?

13. Can you retrieve a file that you inadvertently deleted? What should you do to salvage it?

PROJECTS

PROJECT 1

SPECIFYING COMMANDS

Assume that drive C is the default drive and your system has two floppy disk drives, A and B. Write out the commands you would use to accomplish the following procedures:

1. Format a disk in drive A.
2. List the files on a disk in drive B so that the screen pauses when full.
3. Copy a file named LETTER.91 from drive A to B.
4. Erase all files on drive A that have the extension .BAK.

PROJECT 2

CREATING A DOS REFERENCE CARD

Complete the table "Summary of DOS Commands" by entering in the Command column the command you would use to perform each of the tasks. In the Type column, indicate if the command is an internal or external command.

SUMMARY OF DOS COMMANDS

Description	Command	Type
Formatting Disks		
Formats a data disk in drive A	_____	_____
Formats a data disk and adds a volume label	_____	_____
Adds a volume label to any disk	_____	_____
Formats a system disk in drive A	_____	_____
Displaying Lists of Files		
Lists the files on drive A	_____	_____
Lists all files on drive B with a .DOC extension	_____	_____
Wildcards		
Stands for any single character	_____	_____
Stands for any group of characters	_____	_____
Copying Files		
Copies individual files	_____	_____
Copies all files from drive A to B	_____	_____
Renaming and Erasing Files		
Renames files	_____	_____
Deletes files	_____	_____

Directories & Paths

Using Directories

File Drawers

Directories are a way to organize electronic files on a disk, just as paper files are easier to work with when organized in filing cabinets.

Unorganized file drawers make it difficult to find files when you need them.

Organized file drawers make it easy to find the files you want.

After completing this topic, you will be able to:
- Explain how disks can be organized into directories and subdirectories
- Change directories
- Display lists of directories and files

Dividing a disk into directories helps you organize your files better. Imagine using a file drawer to store all of your memos, letters, and reports. Before long, the drawer would become so crowded and disorganized that you could not find anything. But with a little organization and planning, the documents could be organized into folders, making it easier to locate the one you needed.

A hard disk is like an empty drawer in a new filing cabinet: It provides a lot of storage space but no organization. To make it easier to find items in the drawer, you can divide it into categories with hanging folders. You can file documents directly into the hanging folders, or you can divide them into finer categories with manila folders. A directory is like a hanging folder, and a subdirectory is like a manila folder within a hanging folder. A file in a directory or subdirectory is like a letter, report, or other document within either a hanging folder or a manila folder.

Directories on a hard disk drive are organized in a hierarchy. The main directory, the one not below any other directory, is the root directory. Below it, directories can be created on one or more levels. These directories can hold files or subdirectories. The terms *directory* and *subdirectory* are used somewhat loosely. Strictly speaking, there is only one directory—the root directory—and all others are subdirectories. In most discussions, however, any directory above another is called a directory, and those below it are called its subdirectories.

▶ TUTORIAL

In this tutorial, you explore changing directories on the original *Student Resource Disk.*

GETTING STARTED

1. Load DOS so that the command prompt is displayed.

2. Insert your disks as follows:
   - On a hard disk system, insert the *Student Resource Disk* into drive A.
   - On a floppy disk system, insert the disk with the DOS file TREE.COM into drive A and the *Student Resource Disk* into drive B.
3. Set your drives as follows:
   - On a hard disk system, make drive A the default drive.
   - On a floppy disk system, make drive B the default drive.
4. Type **PROMPT PG** and press [Enter←] so that the prompt indicates the current drive and directory.

CHANGING THE CURRENT DIRECTORY

5. Type **DIR** and press [Enter←] to list all the files on the disk.
6. Type **DIR *.** and press [Enter←] to display just directories off the current directory. On this disk, there are four directories, each followed by *<DIR>*.
7. Type **CD\1-2-3** and press [Enter←] to make the 1-2-3 directory the current directory, and the command prompt reads *A:\1-2-3* or *B:\1-2-3*.
8. Type **DIR** and press [Enter←] to see that the 1-2-3 directory contains a subdirectory named *OLD<DIR>*. The two *<DIR>*s listed next to the periods indicate hidden files and can be ignored.

MOVING BETWEEN DIRECTORIES

9. Type **CD OLD** and press [Enter←] to move down one level, and the prompt now reads *A:\1-2-3\OLD>* or *B:\1-2-3\OLD>*. This indicates that you are in a subdirectory named OLD below the directory named 1-2-3, which is below the root directory A:\ or B:\.
10. Type **CD..** and press [Enter←] to move up one level, and the prompt now reads *A:\1-2-3>* or *B:\1-2-3>*.
11. Type **CD** and press [Enter←] to return to the root directory, and the prompt now reads *A:\>* or *B:\>*.

DISPLAYING A LIST OF DIRECTORIES AND FILES

12. Enter a command as follows:
    - On a hard disk system, type **TREE A:** and press [Enter←].
    - On a floppy disk system, type **A:TREE B:** and press [Enter←].
    A list of the directories is displayed. DOS 4 and later versions show them graphically whereas DOS 3 and earlier versions just list them.
13. Enter a command as follows:
    - On a hard disk system, type **TREE A:/F** and press [Enter←].
    - On a floppy disk system, type **A:TREE B:/F** and press [Enter←].
    Both the directories and the files on the disk are displayed. Notice how when you execute this command, the files cannot all be displayed on the screen at the same time.
14. Press [F3] and then [Enter←] to repeat the command. Press [Ctrl]-[S] or [Pause] to pause the screen display at any point. Press any key to

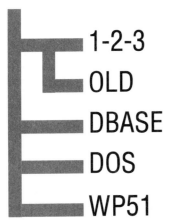

1-2-3
OLD
DBASE
DOS
WP51

The Student Resource Disk Directories
The *Student Resource Disk* directories are organized as shown here.

resume scrolling. Practice these commands until you can pause the screen before all the files scroll past.

FINISHING UP

15. Either continue to the next activity or quit for the day.

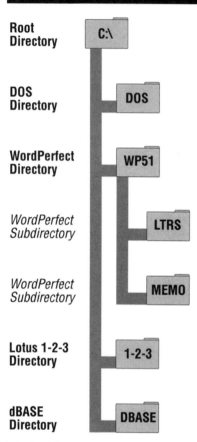

Root Directory — C:\

DOS Directory — DOS

WordPerfect Directory — WP51

WordPerfect Subdirectory — LTRS

WordPerfect Subdirectory — MEMO

Lotus 1-2-3 Directory — 1-2-3

dBASE Directory — DBASE

Directory Trees
Directories and subdirectories are organized into a treelike hierarchy. The topmost directory is called the root directory. Directories below the root directory are called directories. When directories are subdivided into additional directories, they are called subdirectories.

Any disk may be divided into directories and subdirectories. You will often find floppy disks with directories, and almost every hard disk has them. To work with these disks, you have to know how to move between directories and see how they are organized.

Changing Directories
To change directories on the current drive, you use the CHDIR or CD command. To change the default directory, type **CD**<*drive:\directory*> and press [Enter←]. If you are changing more than one level, list the directories in order, separated by a backslash. There are several versions of these commands. For example, in the figure "Moving Through Directories," the following commands would work:

■ To make the subdirectory OLD the default directory, you would type **CD\LETTERS\OLD** and press [Enter←].
■ To move up one directory, for example, from OLD to LETTERS, you would type **CD..** and press [Enter←].
■ To move down to a subdirectory within the current directory, for example, from LETTERS to NEW, you would type **CD NEW**.
■ To return to the root directory from any other directory, you would type **CD** and press [Enter←].

To display the default directory on the current drive, type **CD** and press [Enter←]. To display the current default directory on another drive, type **CD** followed by the drive identifier, and press [Enter←]. For example, to display the current directory on drive C, type **CD C:** and press [Enter←].

→ K E Y / S t r o k e s

Changing Directories

■ To move to a directory, type **CD**<*directory*> and press [Enter←].
■ To return to the root directory, type **CD** and press [Enter←].
■ To move up one level, type **CD..** and press [Enter←].
■ To move down one level, type **CD** <*directory*> and press [Enter←].
■ To display the current directory, type **CD** and press [Enter←].
■ To display the default directory on drive C, type **CD C:** and press [Enter←].

Displaying Files
To list your hard disk's organization, you use the TREE command (an external command). For a list of the directories and the files they

contain, you use the /F switch: TREE/F. This command, unlike the DIR command, lists files in all directories.

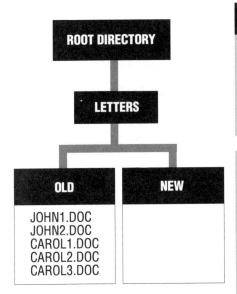

Moving Through Directories
This figure shows the root directory, a LETTERS directory, and two subdirectories, OLD and NEW.

Listing Directories and Files

- To display a list of directories, type **TREE** and press Enter↵ .
- To display a list of directories and the files they contain, type **TREE/F** and press Enter↵ .

TIPS

- When you change the default directory on one drive, and then change default drives, the directory on the previous drive remains set as the default for that drive. When you switch back to that drive, you return to that directory. If you copy files to that drive without specifying otherwise, they are copied to the current default directory.
- Most directory and file management commands work only within the current directory. For example, if you used the ERASE *.* command in a subdirectory, it would erase files only in that subdirectory, not on the entire disk.

> E X E R C I S E

EXERCISE 1

PRINTING A DIRECTORY TREE

1. Use the TREE command to display the tree for the original *Student Resource Disk*.
2. Use the TREE/F command to display the directories and files on the same disk.
3. Describe how the two commands differ.

Making and Removing Directories

After completing this topic, you will be able to:
- Make directories on your own disks
- Remove directories on your own disks

To organize your work on a hard disk drive, you create directories. When the directories are no longer needed, you remove them (after deleting all the files they contain). When creating directories, you should have a plan.

- Keep only essential files in the root directory.
- Store all program files related to a program in their own directory. For example, you might want a directory for DOS, 1-2-3, WordPerfect, and dBASE.
- Do not store the data files that you create in the same directory as the program files. Keep all related data files in their own directories. For example, you might have separate directories for letters, reports, financial documents, and name and address lists. You might also create separate directories for the files you create with different programs. For example, you might have separate directories for WordPerfect documents, 1-2-3 worksheets, or dBASE database files.
- Do not create too many levels since it takes time to move around them. Most disks can be well organized with no more than three levels, including the root directory.

▶ TUTORIAL

In this tutorial, you create and remove subdirectories on the disk labeled *Resource Disk—Backup*.

GETTING STARTED

1. Load DOS so the command prompt is displayed.
2. Insert the disk labeled *Resource Disk—Backup* into drive A, and make that the default drive.
3. Type **PROMPT PG** and press Enter↵ so that the prompt will indicate the drive and directory that you are in.

LETTERS
OLD
NEW
MEMOS
REPORTS

The Student Resource Disk—Backup Directories
This figure shows the organization of the directories and subdirectories that you create and remove in this tutorial.

CREATING DIRECTORIES

4. Type **MD\LETTERS** and press [Enter ←] to create a directory named LETTERS.
5. Type **MD\MEMOS** and press [Enter ←] to create a directory named MEMOS.
6. Type **MD\REPORTS** and press [Enter ←] to create a directory named REPORTS.
7. Type **DIR *.** and press [Enter ←] to see that the three new directories are listed.

CREATING SUBDIRECTORIES

8. Type **MD\LETTERS\NEW** and press [Enter ←] to create a subdirectory named NEW below the directory named LETTERS.
9. Type **MD\LETTERS\OLD** and press [Enter ←] to create a subdirectory named OLD below the directory named LETTERS.

MOVING DOWN THROUGH DIRECTORIES

10. Type **CD\LETTERS** and press [Enter ←] to move down to the LETTERS directory, and the prompt reads *A:\LETTERS>*.
11. Type **DIR** and press [Enter ←] to see that the directory contains the two new subdirectories, NEW and OLD.
12. Type **CD NEW** and press [Enter ←] to move down to the NEW subdirectory, and the prompt reads *A:\LETTERS\NEW>*.

MOVING UP THROUGH DIRECTORIES

13. Type **CD..** and press [Enter ←] to move up one level, and the prompt reads *A:\LETTERS>* to indicate that you have moved up to the LETTERS directory.
14. Type **CD** and press [Enter ←] to return to the root directory, and the prompt now reads *A:\>*.

JUMPING BETWEEN DIRECTORIES

15. Type **CD\LETTERS\NEW** and press [Enter ←] to move down to the NEW subdirectory in one step.
16. Type **CD\LETTERS\OLD** and press [Enter ←] to move directly to the OLD subdirectory.
17. Type **CD..** and press [Enter ←] to move up one level to the LETTERS directory.
18. Type **CD NEW** and press [Enter ←] to move back down to the NEW subdirectory.

REMOVING DIRECTORIES

19. Type **CD** and press [Enter ←] to move back up to the root directory in one step.
20. Type **RD\LETTERS** and press [Enter ←] to remove the LETTERS directory, and a message indicates that you cannot do so because the current directory is not empty. (It still contains subdirectories.)
21. Type **RD\LETTERS\NEW** and press [Enter ←] to remove the NEW subdirectory.

22. Type **RD\LETTERS\OLD** and press ⌷Enter↵⌷ to remove the OLD subdirectory.
23. Type **RD\LETTERS** and press ⌷Enter↵⌷ to remove the LETTERS directory.
24. Type **RD\MEMOS** and press ⌷Enter↵⌷ to remove the MEMOS directory.
25. Type **RD\REPORTS** and press ⌷Enter↵⌷ to remove the REPORTS directory.
26. Type **DIR *.** and press ⌷Enter↵⌷. The message reads *File not found* because there are no directories.

FINISHING UP

27. Either continue to the next activity or quit for the day.

QUICK REFERENCE

To organize your disk, you need to make and remove directories.

Making Directories

To make a directory, you use the internal command MKDIR <*directory name*> (or MD <*directory name*>). Directory names follow the same conventions that you use for filenames. However, you should not use a period and extension, or you might confuse directories with filenames at some later date. Files and subdirectories in one directory can have the same names as files and subdirectories in other directories.

The form of the command depends on whether you are working in the directory below which you want to make a directory or subdirectory. For example, if you wanted to create the directories shown in the figure "Making Directories," you would type:

Making Directories
This tree shows the root directory, a LETTERS, MEMOS, and REPORTS directory, and two subdirectories of the LETTERS directory, NEW and OLD.

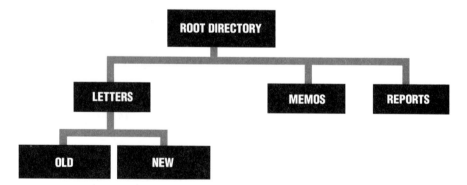

- **MD\LETTERS** and press ⌷Enter↵⌷
- **MD\MEMOS** and press ⌷Enter↵⌷
- **MD\REPORTS** and press ⌷Enter↵⌷

To make the two subdirectories off the LETTERS directory, you would type:

- **MD\LETTERS\NEW** and press ⌷Enter↵⌷
- **MD\LETTERS\OLD** and press ⌷Enter↵⌷

If you had first changed directories so that LETTERS was the default directory, you could make the two subdirectories by typing:

- **MD NEW** and pressing [Enter ←]
- **MD OLD** and pressing [Enter ←]

Making Directories

- To create a directory below the root directory regardless of the directory you are in, type **MD** <directory name>.
- To create a directory below the root directory of another drive, type **MD** <drive:\directory name>. For example, to create a directory named 1-2-3 on drive C when drive B is the default drive, type **MD C:\1-2-3** and press [Enter ←].
- To create a subdirectory in the current directory, type **MD** <directory name>. For example, to create a subdirectory named BUDGETS below the 1-2-3 directory when 1-2-3 is the current default directory, type **MD BUDGETS** and press [Enter ←].

Removing Directories

To remove a directory, you use the internal command RMDIR <directory name> (or RD <directory name>). For example, to delete a directory named LETTERS, you would type **RD LETTERS** and press [Enter ←]. To delete a subdirectory named NEW below a directory named LETTERS, you would type **RD LETTERS\NEW** and press [Enter ←]. The directory you want to remove must not contain any files or subdirectories, and it cannot be the current default directory.

► E X E R C I S E

EXERCISE 1

CREATING AND DELETING DIRECTORIES

1. Insert the disk labeled *Resource Disk—Backup* into one of the disk drives, and make it the default drive.
2. Create a directory named 1992.
3. Create two subdirectories in the 1992 directory named SALES and BUDGETS.
4. Display a tree of the directories.
5. Delete all the new directories and subdirectories from the disk.
6. Display another tree of the directories.

Specifying Paths

After completing this topic, you will be able to:
■ Explain what a path is
■ Specify paths in your own commands
■ Use the XCOPY command with paths to copy files in subdirectories

In previous topics, you frequently specified source and target drives when executing commands that copied, moved, or deleted files. When a disk is divided into directories, you not only must specify a drive, you also must specify a directory or directories in many commands. Specifying the drive and directories is called specifying a path.

Paths are simply a listing of the directories and subdirectories that specify exactly where a file can be found or where it is to be copied to. It is like telling someone that "the letter to ACME Hardware is in the manila folder labeled ACME in the hanging folder labeled Hardware in the third file cabinet from the right." These precise instructions make it easy to locate the file.

▶ T U T O R I A L

In this tutorial, you use paths to copy files on the *Resource Disk— Backup*.

GETTING STARTED

1. Load DOS so that the command prompt is displayed.
2. Insert the disk labeled *Resource Disk—Backup* into drive A, and make that the default drive.

CREATING DIRECTORIES

3. Type **MD\WP51** and press [Enter←].
4. Type **MD\TEXT** and press [Enter←].
5. Type **MD\TEXT\BATCH** and press [Enter←].
6. Type **DIR *.** and press [Enter←] to display the new directories but not the BATCH subdirectory.

COPYING FILES

7. Type **COPY A:CHPT?.WP5 A :\WP51** and press [Enter←] to copy the files into the WP51 directory.

■ ■ ■ ■ ■ ■ ■ ■

8. Type **DIR A:\WP51** and press Enter⏎ to see that the files were copied into the WP51 directory.

9. Type **COPY A:*.TXT A:\TEXT** and press Enter⏎ to copy the files into the TEXT directory.

10. Type **DIR A:\TEXT** and press Enter⏎ to see that the files were copied into the TEXT directory.

11. Type **COPY A:*.BAT A:\TEXT\BATCH** and press Enter⏎ to copy the files into the BATCH subdirectory below the TEXT directory.

12. Type **DIR A:\TEXT\BATCH** and press Enter⏎ to see that the files were copied into the BATCH subdirectory.

ERASING FILES IN THE WP51 DIRECTORY

13. Type **DIR A:\WP51*.*** and press Enter⏎ to preview which files would be deleted with the path and filename specification.

14. Type **ERASE A:\WP51*.*** and press Enter⏎. In a few moments, the prompt reads *Are you sure (Y/N)?*.

15. Press Y and then Enter⏎ to delete the files.

16. Type **DIR A:\WP51** and press Enter⏎ to see that the directory is now empty. The two listings, . *<DIR>* and .. *<DIR>*, indicate hidden files.

ERASING FILES IN THE TEXT DIRECTORY

17. Type **DIR A:\TEXT*.*** and press Enter⏎ to preview which files would be deleted with the path and filename specification.

18. Type **ERASE A:\TEXT*.*** and press Enter⏎. In a few moments, the prompt reads *Are you sure (Y/N)?*.

19. Press Y and then Enter⏎ to delete the files.

20. Type **DIR A:\TEXT** and press Enter⏎ to see that the directory is now empty except for the BATCH subdirectory.

ERASING FILES IN THE BATCH SUBDIRECTORY

21. Type **DIR A:\TEXT\BATCH*.*** and press Enter⏎ to preview which files would be deleted with the path and filename specification.

22. Type **ERASE A:\TEXT\BATCH*.*** and press Enter⏎. In a few moments, the prompt reads *Are you sure (Y/N)?*.

23. Press Y and then Enter⏎ to delete the files.

24. Type **DIR A:\TEXT\BATCH** and press Enter⏎ to see that the directory is now empty. The two listings, . *<DIR>* and .. *<DIR>*, indicate hidden files.

FINISHING UP

25. Either continue to the next activity or quit for the day.

▶ QUICK REFERENCE

To specify a path, you must indicate the drive, then the name of all subdirectories leading to the file, and then the filename. All elements

■   ■   ■   ■   ■   ■   ■   ■

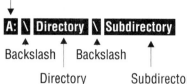

Drive Identifier

A:\ Directory \ Subdirectory

Backslash   Backslash

Directory   Subdirectory
Name   Name

Specifying Paths
When specifying a path, you use a drive identifier and then list a directory and any subdirectories. Each item is separated from the next by a backslash.

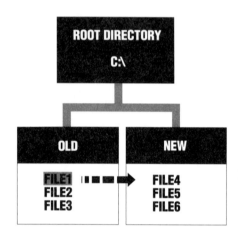

COPY C:\OLD\FILE1 C:\NEW

Paths
When copying files, displaying directories, or deleting files from the command prompt, you have to specify a path when the source or target directory is not the default.

must be separated from one another by backslashes (\), for example, C:\LETTER\NEW\FILE1.DOC.

When specifying paths, you have to consider both the source and target directories:

- If the source directory is the default, you have to specify only the source filename and the path to the target.
- If the target directory is the default, you have to specify only the path to the source and the source filename.
- If neither the target nor the source directory is the default, you have to specify the path for both.

For example, let's assume your disk has the directories and files shown in the figure "Paths."

- To copy files, you have to specify a path only when the source or target directory is not the default.
  - When OLD is the default, the path you specify to copy FILE1 to the NEW directory is only for the target. For example, type **COPY FILE1 C:\NEW**.
  - When NEW is the default, the path you specify to copy FILE1 to the NEW directory is only for the source. For example, type **COPY C:\OLD\FILE1**.
  - When the root directory is the default, the paths you specify to copy FILE1 to the NEW directory are for both the source and the target. For example, type **COPY C:\OLD\FILE1 C:\NEW**.
- To display a list of the filenames in a directory, the same principles work.
  - When the root directory is the default, you can display its directory by just typing **DIR** and pressing [Enter←].
  - To display the files in the OLD directory, you type **DIR C:\OLD** and press [Enter←].
  - To display the files in the NEW directory, you type **DIR C:\NEW** and press [Enter←].
- To delete a file, the same principles also work. For example, when OLD is the default directory:
  - To delete FILE1, you type **DEL FILE1** and press [Enter←].
  - To delete FILE4 in the NEW subdirectory, you type **DEL C:\NEW\FILE4** and press [Enter←].

The XCOPY Command
Your can use the XCOPY command to copy files in subdirectories, files created after a certain date, or only files that weren't copied previously using the switches described in the table "XCOPY Switches." For example:

- To copy all files on a disk in drive C to a disk in drive A, type **XCOPY C:\ A:\/S**.
- To copy all files in the 1-2-3 directory on drive C, and all its subdirectories, to a disk in drive A, type **XCOPY C:\1-2-3 A:/S**.
- To copy just the files in the root directory on the disk in drive C to a disk in drive A, type **XCOPY C:\ A:**.
- To copy just the files in the 1-2-3 directory on drive C, without copying files in any of its subdirectories, type **XCOPY C:\1-2-3 A:**.

When you create a file, DOS sets one of its bits—the archive bit—to 1 to indicate that it is a new file. If you then copy the file with the XCOPY command using the /M switch, DOS changes the archive bit to 0, to indicate that the file has been copied. If you later revise the file and save it again, DOS changes the archive bit back to 1, to show that it is a new file. This property of the /M switch means that you can use it repeatedly and have DOS XCOPY only those files that have not been changed since the last time you used it, ignoring all files that it has previously copied.

If you want to change the archive bit back from 0 to 1 manually, you can do it with the ATTRIB *<filename or wildcard>* +A command. For example, to reset the archive bit to 1 for every file in the current directory with the extension .DOC, type **ATTRIB *.DOC +A** and press [Enter←].

■ To copy all files on a disk in drive C, with a date later than December 31, 1992, to a disk in drive A, type **XCOPY C:\ A:\/S/ D:12-31-92**.
■ To copy all files on a disk in drive C that have been changed since you last used the XCOPY command to a disk in drive A, type **XCOPY C:\ A:\/S/M**.

XCOPY SWITCHES

Switch	Description
/P	Prompts you before copying each file.
/D:mm-dd-yy	Copies only files created on or after the specified date.
/W	Waits for you to insert a disk and press any key before copying.
/S	Copies all files in the source directory and its subdirectories.
/E	Creates subdirectories on the target to match those on the source.
/V	Verifies that files are copied correctly.
/M	Copies only those files whose archive bit is 1; after the file has been copied, the archive bit for the source file is set to 0. (The archive bit is a marker that indicates if a file has been backed up or not.) When using this switch, the source disk cannot be write-protected.
/A	Same as /M but does not change the archive bit for the source file.

XCOPY with the /M switch is very useful for copying files when the target disk does not have enough room for all the files on the source. Say you want to copy all the files in the 123 directory of drive C to a disk in drive A but a disk in that drive won't hold all of them. Type **XCOPY C: \123 A: /M**. When the first disk is full, the message *Insufficient disk space* is displayed and the command prompt reappears. Put a new floppy into the drive and repeat the XCOPY command (press [F3]). XCOPY will copy another diskful of files, but it will not copy any files it has already copied, because the /M switch changed their archive bit to 0 after copying them. Continue to do this until all the files have been copied and the command prompt reappears without the *Insufficient disk space* message. If you want XCOPY to copy the files in subdirectories of the source directory too with this procedure, remember to use the /S switch along with the /M one. If you want it to create subdirectories to match those of the source disk even if those subdirectories are empty, use the /E switch too.

►EXERCISE

EXERCISE 1

PRINTING DIRECTORIES

1. Insert the *Student Resource Disk* into drive A.
2. Change the default drive to A.
3. Without changing the default directory, use the DIR command to display a directory of all the files in the root directory and the subdirectories on the disk.

■　■　■　■　■　■　■　■

REVIEW

- A disk can be divided into directories and subdirectories. The highest-level directory is called the root directory.
- To change directories, you use the CD or CHDIR command. For example, to change to a directory named LETTERS, you type **CD\LETTERS** and press Enter↵.
- To display a list of directories on a hard disk drive, you use the TREE command. To display a list of directories and the files they contain, you use the TREE/F command.
- The command you use to make new directories on a disk is MKDIR (or MD), which is an internal command.
- The command you use to remove a directory is RD or RMDIR, which is an internal command. You can remove a directory only if it is empty—that is, it can't contain files or subdirectories.
- To specify a path, you specify the drive and any directories between the root directory and the file. For example, to copy a file named FILENAME on drive C from the directory LETTERS to the directory MEMOS, type **COPY C:\LETTERS\FILENAME C:\MEMOS**.

QUESTIONS

FILL IN THE BLANK

1. To move to a directory named LETTERS on drive C, you would enter the command _____.
2. To move to a directory named OLD below a directory named LETTERS on drive C, you would enter the command _____.
3. To move back to the root directory from any subdirectory, you would enter the command _____.
4. To move up one level in the directory tree, you would enter the command _____.
5. To create a directory named LETTERS on drive C, you would enter the command _____.
6. To create a directory named OLD below a directory named LETTERS on drive C, you would enter the command _____.
7. To remove a directory named LETTERS on drive C, you would enter the command _____.
8. To remove a directory named OLD below a directory named LETTERS on drive C, you would enter the command _____.
9. To copy a file named JOHN.DOC to a directory named LETTERS on drive C, you would enter the command _____.

10. To copy a file named JOHN.DOC to a directory named OLD below a directory named LETTERS on drive C, you would enter the command _____.

MATCH THE COLUMNS

1. CD\
2. CD ..
3. <DIR>
4. [1-2-3]
5. TREE
6. TREE/F
7. MD
8. RD
9. C:\TEXT\BATCH

___ Indicates a directory when you use the DIR/W command

___ Displays a list of directories, subdirectories, and files

___ Returns you to the root directory

___ A path to a subdirectory on drive C

___ Makes a directory

___ Indicates a directory when you use the DIR command

___ Moves you up one level in the directories

___ Displays a list of directories and subdirectories

___ Removes a directory

WRITE OUT THE ANSWERS

1. What is the topmost directory on a disk called?

2. What command do you use to change directories? What command do you use to move up one level? Are these internal or external commands?

3. What must you do before you can remove a directory from a hard disk?

4. What command do you use when you want to display the directories on a hard disk? When you want to display both the directories and the files?

5. What command do you use to make directories?

6. What command do you use to remove directories?

7. If you wanted to create a directory named FIRST below the root directory, what command would you use?

8. If you wanted to create a subdirectory named SECOND below the directory named FIRST, what command would you use?

9. If the SECOND directory was the current default directory, what two commands could you use to create a new subdirectory below it named THIRD?

10. To copy a file named JONES from the root directory of drive A to a directory named LETTERS on drive C, what command would you use?

11. To display a listing of the files in a subdirectory named SECOND below a directory named FIRST, what command would you use from the root directory?

PROJECTS

PROJECT 1

PLANNING AND DRAWING A DIRECTORY TREE

Sketch out a directory tree for the following directories and subdirectories. Name each of the directories and subdirectories as you see fit.

1. The root directory is drive C.
2. Below the root directory are directories for DOS, Lotus 1-2-3, WordPerfect 5.1, dBASE III Plus, budgets, reports, memos, and letters.
3. Below the budgets, reports, memos, and letters directories are subdirectories for 1993, 1994, and 1995.

PROJECT 2

CREATING A DOS REFERENCE CARD

The table "Summary of DOS Commands" lists some of the most frequently used DOS command procedures. Complete the table by entering in the Command column the command you would use to perform each of the tasks. In the Type column, indicate if the command is an internal or external command.

SUMMARY OF DOS COMMANDS

Description	Command	Type
Making and Changing Directories		
Creates a new directory	_____	_____
Changes the default directory	_____	_____
Removes a directory	_____	_____
Returns to the root directory	_____	_____
Returns to one level up	_____	_____
Displays a list of directories	_____	_____
Displays a list of directories and files	_____	_____

Advanced DOS Procedures

Checking Disks and Files

After completing this topic, you will be able to:
- Explain why disks should be checked periodically
- Check disks and files on your own system

When you save a file on a new disk, it is stored neatly on adjacent sectors around adjacent tracks on the disk. But after the disk begins to fill up and you delete some files and add others, the disk drive has to work harder to store a file. It tends to store different parts of the file wherever it can find free sectors. After a while, a file may end up scattered all over the disk on noncontiguous blocks (parts of the file that do not adjoin each other on the disk). Files stored this way are called fragmented files.

When files are stored in widely separated sectors, some blocks may get lost and not be retrievable. Moreover, the drive's read/write head will have to move back and forth more frequently. This puts increased wear and tear on the drive because the drive's read/write head must keep moving over the disk's surface to reach parts of the files. It also slows down any save and retrieve operations.

To determine if files are fragmented, use the CHKDSK command. To correct the disk, copy all files onto another disk using the COPY *.* command. If the disk contains subdirectories, use the XCOPY command with the /S switch.

B:\PART1.DOC
Contains 3 non-contiguous blocks
B:\PART2.DOC
Contains 2 non-contiguous blocks

The CHKDSK Command
If you use the CHKDSK *.* command and get a message that your disk contains noncontiguous blocks, you need to unfragment your disk.

► TUTORIAL

In this tutorial, you check the disk labeled *Resource Disk—Backup*.

GETTING STARTED

1. Load DOS so that the command prompt is displayed.
2. Insert your disks as follows:
   - On a hard disk system, insert the disk labeled *Resource Disk— Backup* into drive A.
   - On a floppy disk system, insert the disk that contains the CHKDSK.COM or CHKDSK.EXE file into drive A and the disk labeled *Resource Disk—Backup* into drive B.

3. Set your drives as follows:
  - On a hard disk system, make drive C the default drive.
  - On a floppy disk system, make drive A the default drive.

CHECKING A DISK

4. Enter a command as follows:
  - On a hard disk system, type **CHKDSK A:** and press [Enter⏎].
  - On a floppy disk system, type **CHKDSK B:** and press [Enter⏎].

When you use this command, the screen indicates the following information about your system:

  - The total disk space, the space allocated to data files, and the remaining space available on the disk
  - The size and number of hidden files (if any)
  - The size and number of directories
  - The size and number of user files
  - If you are using DOS 4 or 5, the number of bytes in each allocation unit, the total number of allocation units, and the remaining allocation units available for new files
  - The total memory in the computer and the amount that is currently free (not occupied by programs or data)

CHECKING THE FILES ON A DISK

5. Enter a command as follows:
  - On a hard disk system, type **CHKDSK A:*.*** and press [Enter⏎].
  - On a floppy disk system, type **CHKDSK B:*.*** and press [Enter⏎].

If all the files on the disk are contiguous, a message reads *All specified file(s) are contiguous*. If some are not, a series of messages tells you which files contain noncontiguous blocks.

FINISHING UP

6. Either continue to the next activity or quit for the day.

QUICK REFERENCE

To check a disk, you use the CHKDSK command (an external command). You can also use variations of the CHKDSK command to check individual files. For example:

  - To check a single file, type **CHKDSK B:<*filename*>** (where <*filename*>is the name of the file).
  - To list the names of files as they are being checked, use the /V switch. For example, to list the names of all files on drive B as they are being checked, type **CHKDSK B:/V**.
  - To check the status of all files on a disk, type **CHKDSK B:*.*** and press [Enter⏎]. This command gives you the same information as the other CHKDSK commands but also tells you if all files occupy contiguous, or adjacent, blocks (as they should) or lists the files

Contiguous and Noncontiguous Sectors

Disks with files located in contiguous sectors put less wear and tear on the drive and allow faster file saving and retrieving.

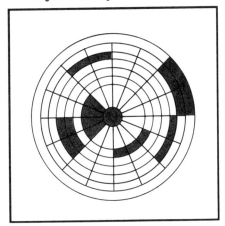

When a file is stored in noncontiguous sectors, parts of it are scattered about the disk. For the disk drive to retrieve such a file, it must move back and forth all over the disk.

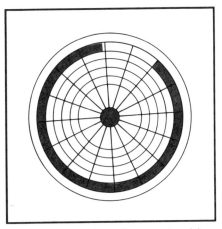

When a file is stored in contiguous sectors, it is stored on the disk in adjacent sectors. The disk drive can retrieve such a file in one smooth, continuous operation.

that contain noncontiguous, or scattered, blocks as shown in the figure "The CHKDSK Command."

If your disk contains noncontiguous blocks, you should copy the files to a new disk so that they are contiguous. To do so, copy all the files to a new formatted disk with the COPY *.* or XCOPY /S command. You can also use utility programs such as Norton Ulitities to move files together into contiguous sectors. This is the only practical way to do it on hard disks.

→ **KEY / Strokes**

Checking the Files on a Disk

1. On a floppy disk system, insert the DOS disk that contains the CHKDSK.COM or CHKDSK.EXE file into drive A, and make that the default drive.
2. Insert your disks as follows:
   ■ On a hard disk system, insert the disk you want to check into drive A.
   ■ On a floppy disk system, insert the disk you want to check into drive B.
3. Enter one of the following commands:
   ■ On a hard disk system, type:
      • **CHKDSK A:** and press [Enter ←] to check the disk
      • **CHKDSK A*.*** and press [Enter ←] to check files on the disk
      • **CHKDSK A:/V** and press [Enter ←] to list files as they are checked
   ■ On a floppy disk system, type:
      • **CHKDSK B:** and press [Enter ←] to check the disk
      • **CHKDSK B*.*** and press [Enter ←] to check files on the disk
      • **CHKDSK B:/V** and press [Enter ←] to list files as they are checked

TIPS

■ If sectors of a file become scattered, the operating system may not be able to find sections called allocation units, or blocks. The CHKDSK command occasionally displays the following message:

> Errors found, F parameter not specified
> Corrections will not be written to disk
>
> Convert lost chains to files (Y/N)?
>   4096 bytes disk space would be freed

■ If you see this message, press [N] and then [Enter ←] to return to the command prompt. Type **CHKDSK /F** and press [Enter ←]. When the message reappears, press [Y] and then [Enter ←] to store the lost allocation units in one or more files named

FILEnnnn.CHK (where nnnn is a sequential number) in the root directory. You can then retrieve these files to see if any contain useful data that you want to recover. You can retrieve these files with any application program that reads ASCII text files, or you can see their contents with the command TYPE FILE<*nnnn*>.CHK or TYPE FILE<*nnnn*>.CHK I MORE.

▶ E X E R C I S E

EXERCISE 1

CHECKING DISKS

Check any of your disks with the CHKDSK, CHKDSK *.*, and CHKDSK/ V commands.

Using the DOS 5 Shell

After completing this topic, you will be able to:
- Describe the parts of the DOS Shell
- Use DOS Shell menus to execute commands

DOS 5 contains a built-in Shell that gives you a visual representation of the drives, directories, and files on your system as shown in the figure "The DOS 5 Shell." You can select any of these items and then execute the most frequently used DOS commands on them by making choices from menus like the one shown in the figure "The Shell's Pull-Down Menus." You can also list your own application programs on the Shell's program list so that you can run them directly from the Shell.

The DOS 5 Shell

The DOS 5 Shell contains all the elements shown in this figure. However, your screen display may differ from the MS-DOS 5 shell shown here. The Shell can be displayed in character or graphics mode, and the areas shown and the programs listed can be modified. There are also differences between the MS-DOS and IBM-DOS versions of the Shell.

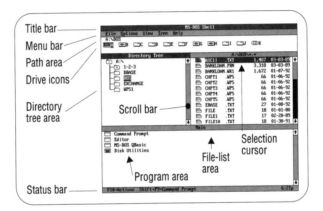

The Shell's screen display is divided into a number of areas, each of which displays a different type of information.

- The *path area* lists the current default path. For example, when it reads *C:*, the current directory is the root directory on drive C. If it reads *C:\DOS*, then DOS is the current directory.
- The *drive icon area* indicates the drives on your system with graphic symbols, called icons. The icon for the current default drive is always highlighted.
- The *directory-tree area* lists directories and subdirectories on the disk in the default drive. The current directory is always highlighted.
- The *file-list area* lists the files in the current directory. When you change the current directory on the directory tree, or select another drive in the drive-icon area, the list of files automatically changes.
- The *program-list area* lists programs that you can run without leaving the Shell.

In addition to these areas, the Shell displays the following items:

- The *menu bar* lists the names of menus that you can pull down to display commands.
- The *selection cursor* is a reverse-video or colored highlight that you move among areas of the screen to select drives, directories, files, or program names.
- A *mouse pointer* is displayed if your system has a mouse and DOS has been set up for it.
- The *status bar* lists messages and keys you can press to execute commands.

The Shell's Pull-Down Menus
When you press Alt or click on the menu bar with the mouse pointer, you can pull down menus listing many DOS commands.

> **T U T O R I A L**

In this tutorial, you use the Shell that is built into DOS 5. As you do so, you select commands from the keyboard, not with a mouse. If your system has a mouse, you can repeat the tutorial using the mouse instead of the keyboard to execute commands.

GETTING STARTED

1. Load DOS so that the Shell is displayed. If the Shell is not displayed automatically:
   - On a hard disk system, type **DOSSHELL** and press Enter←.
   - On a floppy disk system, insert the disk that contains the Shell program into drive A, type **DOSSHELL** and press Enter←.
2. Insert your disks as follows:
   - On a hard disk system, insert the disk labeled *Resource Disk— Backup* into drive A.
   - On a floppy disk system, insert the disk labeled *Resource Disk— Backup* into drive B.

CHANGING DEFAULT DRIVES

3. Press → to move the selection cursor from drive icon to drive icon. (If the selection cursor is not in the drive-icon area of the screen, press Tab⇆ one or more times to move it there.)
4. Select one of the drive icons as follows:

- On a hard disk system, highlight the icon for drive A and press [Enter ←].
- On a floppy disk system, highlight the icon for drive B and press [Enter ←].

EXPLORING HELP

5. Press [Alt] to select the menu bar, and the first letter in each menu name is highlighted.
6. Press [H] (for *Help*), and the Help menu descends from the menu bar.
7. Press [S] (for *Shell Basics*), and a help panel appears that describes Shell basics.
8. Press [↓] or [PgDn] to scroll down through the help text, and press [↑] or [PgUp] to scroll back up. Additional topics on which you can display help are highlighted in color or reverse video.
9. Press [↓] or [↑] to display the list of related help topics. The first topic listed is *Welcome to MS-DOS Shell* (or *Welcome to IBM DOS Shell* on the IBM version of DOS).
10. Press [Tab ⇆] repeatedly to move the selection cursor to the *Index* command button at the bottom of the help window, and press [Enter ←] to display an index of help topics.
11. Scroll through the list, highlight any topic of interest, and press [Enter ←] to display help on it.
12. Continue exploring help until you are comfortable with how it works.
13. When you have finished exploring help, press [Esc] to remove the help panel and return to the Shell.

EXPLORING MENUS WITH ARROW KEYS

14. Press [Alt] to activate the menu bar, and the File menu's name is highlighted.
15. Press [↓] to pull down the File menu, and all available commands are listed.
16. Press [→] to pull down the Options menu.
17. Press [→] to pull down the View menu.
18. Press [→] to pull down the Tree menu.
19. Press [→] to pull down the Help menu.
20. Press [→] to pull down the File menu again.
21. Press [↓] to highlight *Create directory*, and press [Enter ←] to display a dialog box with a space into which you type the name of the new directory.
22. Type **MYDIR** and press [Enter ←] to add a new directory named MYDIR to the menu tree.

EXPLORING MENUS WITH MNEMONIC KEYS

23. Press [Tab ⇆] to move the selection cursor to the Directory Tree and highlight *MYDIR* directory.
24. Press [Alt] and then [F] (for *File*) to pull down the File menu.

25. Press ⃞D (for *Delete*) to remove the highlighted directory from the disk and the directory tree. If the confirmation on delete option is on, a prompt reads *Delete A:\MYDIR?* or *Delete B:\MYDIR?*. If this prompt appears, highlight *Yes* and press ⃞Enter↵ .

RENAMING A FILE

26. Press ⃞Tab⇆ to move the section cursor to the File list.
27. Highlight the file named *WHATSUP.DOC*.
28. Press ⃞Alt to select the menu bar.
29. Press ⃞F (for *File*) to pull down the File menu.
30. Press ⃞N (for *Rename*) to display a dialog box.
31. Type **NEWFILE.DOC** and press ⃞Enter↵ to change the file's name on the File list to NEWFILE.DOC.

COPYING A FILE

32. Highlight the file named NEWFILE.DOC, and press ⃞Alt to select the menu bar.
33. Press ⃞F (for *File*) to pull down the File menu.
34. Press ⃞C (for *Copy*) to display a dialog box.
35. Type **WHATSUP.DOC** and press ⃞Enter↵ to add the filename WHATSUP.DOC to the File list.

ERASING A FILE

36. Highlight the file named *NEWFILE.DOC*.
37. Press ⃞Alt to select the menu bar.
38. Press ⃞F (for *File*) to pull down the File menu.
39. Press ⃞D (for *Delete*) to delete the highlighted file from the disk and remove it from the file list. If the confirmation on delete option is on, a prompt reads *Delete A:\NEWFILE.DOC?* or *Delete B:\NEWFILE.DOC?*. If this prompt appears, highlight *Yes* and press ⃞Enter↵ .

FINISHING UP

40. Either continue to the next activity or quit for the day.

▶ Q U I C K   R E F E R E N C E

You can execute the Shell's commands with the keyboard or with a mouse. When doing so, you can display help at any time.

Getting Help

Whenever the Shell is displayed, you can display help by pressing ⃞F1 or by pulling down the Help menu and selecting a topic. Help is context sensitive, which means the help text displayed (called a help panel) depends on the cursor's position. Many help panels have lists of related commands displayed in color or reverse video. You press ⃞Tab⇆ to move a highlight or a small arrow from one of these topics to another. With the topic highlighted or with the small arrow pointing to it, press ⃞Enter↵

to display help on it. To remove the help panel, press Esc. At the bottom of each help panel are command buttons that close the help window, move you back, display help on keys, show an index, or display help on help. To choose one of these, press Tab⇆ to move the selection cursor to the desired button, and press Enter↵. If you are using a mouse, you can click on topics or command buttons to choose them. To do so, you use the mouse to move the mouse pointer on the screen. When the mouse pointer is pointing to the desired topic or button, you click the left button.

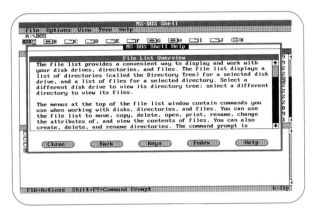

Moving Between Areas of the Shell

When the Shell is loaded, the screen displays the DOS Shell window. This window is divided into a number of areas, each of which displays a different type of information. The areas include those that display drive icons, a directory tree, a file list, and a program list. Commands listed on the View menu govern which of these areas is displayed on your system.

- You move the selection cursor between areas by pressing Tab⇆ or **Backtab**. (Hold down ⇧ Shift and press Tab⇆.)
- You move within areas by pressing the arrow keys.

Using the Shell's Pull-Down Menus

The menu bar contains pull-down menus with the choices listed in the table "The DOS Shell Menu Choices." (The choices on the File menu are different when the selection cursor is in the Program list.)

- To activate and deactivate the menu bar, you press Alt or F10. Once the menu is activated, press → or ← to move between menu choices and then press ↓ to pull down the highlighted menu. You can then press → or ← to pull down other menus.
- If using a mouse, you point to the menu name, and then click to pull it down. The mouse pointer is displayed as a highlighted box (in text mode) or as an arrow (in graphics mode). If you pull down a menu and decide not to make a choice, point to any area outside the menu, and then click the mouse button. The table "Executing Commands with a Mouse" describes the procedures you follow to execute commands with a mouse.

EXECUTING COMMANDS WITH A MOUSE

To	Point To	Click
Pull down a menu	Menu's name	Left button
Start a program	Program's name	Left button twice
Exit a pull-down menu without making a choice	Outside menu	Left button

When the menu bar is activated, you can pull down the menus in three ways:

- By pressing the letter that is underlined or highlighted (called a mnemonic) in the choice's name. For example, you can press F to pull down the File menu or H to pull down the Help menu.
- By using the arrow keys to highlight the name with the selection cursor and pressing Enter← or ↓ to pull down the menu.
- By clicking on the desired menu name with a mouse.

If you do not want to make a selection, press Esc or point with the mouse to another area of the screen and click.

The table "Executing Commands from the Keyboard" summarizes the keys you use to execute menu commands.

EXECUTING COMMANDS FROM THE KEYBOARD

To	Press
Activate or deactivate the menu bar	Alt or F10
Pull down a menu from the activated menu bar	
with arrow keys	← or → and then ↓
with mnemonic keys	Mnemonic letter
Select a choice from a pull-down menu	
with arrow keys	↓ or ↑ and then Enter←
with mnemonic keys	Mnemonic letter
Exit a pull-down menu without making a choice but leave the menu bar activated	Alt or F10
Exit a pull-down menu without making a choice and deactivate the menu bar	Esc
Move the selection cursor between areas of the Shell	Tab↹

The choices on the menu bar provide additional information other than the command they execute.

- Choices on pull-down menus followed by an ellipsis (...) display dialog boxes when selected. Dialog boxes are like on-screen forms that you fill out with information the computer needs.
- Choices on pull-down menus that are dimmed or not listed are not selectable from where you are in the procedure.

THE DOS SHELL MENU CHOICES

Menu	Description
File	
*O*pen	Runs the selected executable program file that ends with the extension .COM, .EXE, or .BAT and opens an associated file if you selected one (see **A**ssociate).
*R*un...	Displays a dialog box in which you enter the name of a program you want to run.
Print	Prints up to ten selected ASCII text files.
Associate...	Links filename extension to programs so that if you select a data file with the specified extension, the associated program is automatically run.
Sear**c**h...	Searches for files that you specify in a dialog box that appears when you select this choice. If you check the *Search entire disk* option, DOS searches the disk in the default drive. If you leave this unchecked, DOS just searches the current directory.
View File Contents	Displays the contents of the selected file.
*M*ove...	Moves selected files to another drive or directory and deletes the original file.
*C*opy...	Copies selected files to another drive or directory or to the current one if you specify a new name in the dialog box.
*D*elete...	Deletes selected files.
Rename...	Renames selected files.
Change Attributes	Changes a selected file's attributes to Hidden, Read-Only, or Archive. (See your DOS manual.)
Create Directory...	Creates a new directory.
Select All	Selects all files in the File List.
Deselect All	Deselects any previously selected files in the File List.
E*x*it	Closes the Shell and displays the command prompt.
Options	
*C*onfirmation...	Turns confirmation prompts on and off for *D*elete, **C**opy, and *M*ove commands; also specifies if files are to be selected in more than one directory or not.
File Display Options...	Displays selected files and sorts files in the File List.
Select **A**cross Directories...	Allows you to select files in more than one directory at the same time so that you can copy, move, or delete them.
Show Information...	Displays information on the highlighted file.
*E*nable Task Swapper	When enabled, you can run more than one program at the same time and switch back and forth between them.
*D*isplay...	Changes the way the Shell is displayed.
Colors...	Changes the colors used in the Shell display.
View	
Single File List	Displays Directory Tree and File List for current drive.
Dual File Lists	Displays Directory Tree and File List for two drives or directories.
All Files	Displays a list of all files on a disk regardless of the directories they are stored in.
Program/**F**ile Lists	Displays Directory Tree and File List for current drive and a list of DOS programs.
*P*rogram List	Displays just a list of DOS programs.

THE DOS SHELL MENU CHOICES (CONTINUED)

Menu	Description
Repaint Screen	Updates the screen display.
Refresh	Updates the list of files after you delete or restore any.
Tree	
Expand One Level	Shows one more level of subdirectories for the selected directory.
Expand Branch	Shows all levels of subdirectories for the selected directory.
Expand All	Shows all levels of subdirectories for all directories.
Collapse Branch	Hides all subdirectories below the selected directory.
Help	
Index	Displays a list of topics on which help is available.
Keyboard	Displays a list of topics on keys you use to execute commands.
Shell Basics	Displays basic help on using the Shell.
Commands	Displays all menu commands so that you can get help on them.
Procedures	Displays a list of procedures you may need help with.
Using Help	Displays help on using help.
About Shell	Displays the version number and copyright information on the Shell.

Responding to Dialog Boxes

All menu choices followed by an ellipsis (...) display dialog boxes when you select them. Dialog boxes are requests for additional information, which you enter into the dialog boxes' text boxes or select from lists. When the text that you type into a text box reaches the right end of the box, the entry scrolls off the screen to the left. If your entry is too long, eventually the computer beeps, and you have to stop typing.

When entering text into text boxes, you can use the following editing commands:

- You can press ← and → to move the cursor through the text. You can also press End to move the cursor to the end of the entry or Home to move it to the beginning.
- If the text box already contains an entry, the first character you type will delete it. If you want to just edit the existing entry, press ← or → before typing any other character, and you will enter edit mode. In this mode, you can then move the cursor through the entry to insert characters or use Del or ←Bksp to delete them.

Changing Default Drives

The drive-icon area lists the drives on your system. The current default drive is highlighted. To change the default drive:

- Press Tab↹ to move the selection cursor to this area, press ← or → to highlight the drive you want to make the default, and press Enter↵. You can also hold down Ctrl and press the letter of the drive when the selection cursor is in the drive-icon area.
- If using a mouse, point to the drive and then click.

As you change the default drive, the path area, the directory tree, and the file list reflect the change.

Changing Default Directories

The directory-tree area lists all directories and subdirectories, if any, on the disk. To change the default directory:

- Press [Tab↹] to move the selection cursor to this area, press [↓] or [↑] to highlight the directory you want to make the default, and press [Enter↵].
- If using a mouse, point to the directory, and then click.

As you change the default directory, the path area and file list reflect the change.

Selecting Files

The file-list area normally lists the files on the default drive and directory. At the top of this area the current file specification is listed. You can change this specification with the *File Display Options* command listed on the Options menu. The default file specification is *.* which displays all the files on the disk.

- If there are too many filenames to be displayed at one time, the list extends off the bottom of the area. To scroll through the list of files, press [Tab↹] to move the selection cursor to this area. You then press [↑], [↓], [PgUp], and [PgDn] to scroll the list. You can also press [Ctrl]-[Home] to move to the top of the list or [Ctrl]-[End] to move to the bottom.
- To select a single file, press [⇧ Shift]-[F8], and *ADD* is displayed on the status bar and the file's icon remains highlighted when you move the selection cursor off it. To unselect a selected file, highlight the file, and press [Spacebar].
- To select files that are adjacent to one another on the list, you select the first filename, and then extend the selection. To do so, highlight the first file you want to select, and then hold down [⇧ Shift] while you press [↑] or [↓] to extend the selection to the other files.
- To select or deselect files that are not adjacent to one another, highlight the first file, and press [⇧ Shift]-[F8]. When you do so, *ADD* is displayed on the status bar, and the file's icon remains highlighted when you move the selection cursor off it. To select additional files, highlight them and press [Spacebar]. After selecting all the files you want, press [⇧ Shift]-[F8] again, and *ADD* disappears from the status bar.
- To select or deselect all files, press [Tab↹] to move the selection cursor to the file-list area, pull down the File menu, and then choose **S**elect all or *Deselect all*.

If your Shell has been installed for a mouse, the arrows or scroll bar can be used instead of [PgUp] and [PgDn] to scroll the file list or directory tree. The scroll bar contains both up and down arrows and a slider box. The slider box indicates which part of the list is currently displayed. To scroll any list:

- Point to the arrows at the top or bottom of the scroll bar, and then click. Hold the mouse button down to scroll continuously.

- Point to the slider box within the scroll bar, hold down the mouse button, and drag the slider box up or down. Release the button to scroll the list to that point.
- To select files that are adjacent to one another on the list, click the first name, and then hold down ⟨⇧ Shift⟩ and click the last name.
- To select or deselect files that are not adjacent to one another, hold down ⟨Ctrl⟩ while you click each filename.

Running Programs

A program list is displayed when you select *Program/File Lists* from the View menu. This area lists programs that you can execute. Some programs are directly listed in this area, but others have been grouped together under a single heading. For example, if you select *Command Prompt* or *Editor* (called *IBM DOS Editor* on IBM's version of DOS 5), the command is immediately executed. However, if you select *Disk Utilities*, another list is displayed. It is from this second list that you actually execute the commands.

The default program list (yours may have been modified) is named Main, and it contains those programs shown in the table "The Program-List Area Commands." To select one of the listed commands, highlight it and press ⟨Enter ←⟩ or double-click it with a mouse. (Click on it twice in rapid succession.)

THE PROGRAM-LIST AREA COMMANDS FOR MS-DOS (DIFFERENT ON IBM VERSION)

Choice	Description
Command Prompt	Displays the command prompt. Type **EXIT** and press ⟨Enter ←⟩ to return to the Shell.
Editor	Displays a dialog box asking you the name of the file that you want to edit.
MS-DOS QBasic	Displays a dialog box asking you the name of the file that you want to run.
Disk Utilities	Displays a list of utility programs you can run. • *Main* returns you to the main program list. • *Disk Copy* makes duplicate disks. • *Backup Fixed Disk* backs up a hard disk onto floppy disks. • *Restore Fixed Disk* restores a hard disk's files from backups on floppy disks. • *Quick Format* formats a disk more quickly if it has already been formatted once. • *Format* formats data and system disks. • *Undelete* recovers deleted files.

When the selection cursor is in the program-list area, the commands listed on the File menu change from those that are normally displayed. These commands are described in the table "File Menu Choices with the Selection Cursor in the Program List."

FILE MENU CHOICES WITH THE SELECTION CURSOR
IN THE PROGRAM LIST

Choice	Description
New...	Adds a program or group of programs to the currently selected group
Open	Runs a program or displays the contents of a group
Copy	Copies a program or group of programs to another group
Delete...	Deletes the selected group or selected item within a group
Properties...	Describes the program to be run
Reorder	Rearranges programs and groups to a different position in the list
Run...	Displays a dialog box in which you enter the name of a program to run
Exit	Closes the Shell and displays the command prompt

► E X E R C I S E

EXERCISE 1

USING THE SHELL'S MENUS

1. Insert your *Resource Disk—Backup* into drive A on a hard disk system or drive B on a floppy disk system.
2. Change the default drive, if necessary, to the drive into which you inserted the disk.
3. Use the Shell's menus to create three directories, SHELL1, SHELL2, and SHELL3.
4. Use the Shell's menus to copy all the files that begin with CHPT to the SHELL1 directory.
5. Use the Shell's menus to copy all the files that begin with FILE to the SHELL2 directory.
6. Use the Shell's menus to copy the WHATSUP.DOC file to the SHELL3 directory.
7. Use the Shell's menus to erase all the files in each directory, and then delete the directories.

REVIEW

- The command you use to check your disks is CHKDSK, an external command. When files are deleted and then new files are saved onto a disk, files that you copy to the disk or save onto it with an application program may be stored in noncontiguous sectors. To find files like this, use the CHKDSK *.* command.
- Because DOS commands can be hard to remember, Shells have been developed that allow you to execute DOS commands by making menu selections. You can display DOS 4 and later Shells by typing **DOSSHELL** at the command prompt.

CHAPTER 4 QUESTIONS

FILL IN THE BLANK

1. To check the disk in drive A, you would enter the command _____.

2. To load the DOS Shell from the command prompt, you would type _____.

MATCH THE COLUMNS

1. CHKDSK   __ Fixes a disk that has lost chains
2. CHKDSK *.*   __ Gives you the status of a disk
3. CHKDSK /V   __ Activates the DOS Shell's menu bar
4. CHKDSK /F   __ Gives you the status of a disk and the files on it
5. DOSSHELL
6. [Alt]   __ Displays the Shell built into DOS 4 and later versions

   __ Lists files as it checks a disk's status

WRITE OUT THE ANSWERS

1. What command do you use to check disks? Is the command an internal or external command?
2. What happens to files, when the disk begins to get full, that makes the drive work harder and take longer to retrieve and save the files?
3. If you get a message telling you your files have noncontiguous sectors, what does it mean?
4. If a disk has noncontiguous sectors, how can you fix the files so that they are all in adjacent sectors on the disk?

5. What is the difference between the CHKDSK and CHKDSK *.* commands?

6. What command do you type to display the DOS Shell from the command prompt?

7. When the DOS Shell is displayed, what key do you press to activate the menu bar?

PROJECT

PROJECT 1

CREATING A DOS REFERENCE CARD

The table "Summary of DOS Commands" lists some of the most frequently used DOS command procedures. Complete the table by entering in the Command column the command you would use to perform each of the tasks. In the Type column, indicate if the command is an internal or external command.

SUMMARY OF DOS COMMANDS

Description	Command	Type
Checking Disks		
Gives status of memory, disk space, and any noncontiguous blocks	_____	_____
Displays each filename as it is checked	_____	_____
Displays a prompt that asks you if you want to correct errors	_____	_____